Candlesticks Forex trading pattern

An Essential Candlestick Patterns For All Traders

Frank Luther

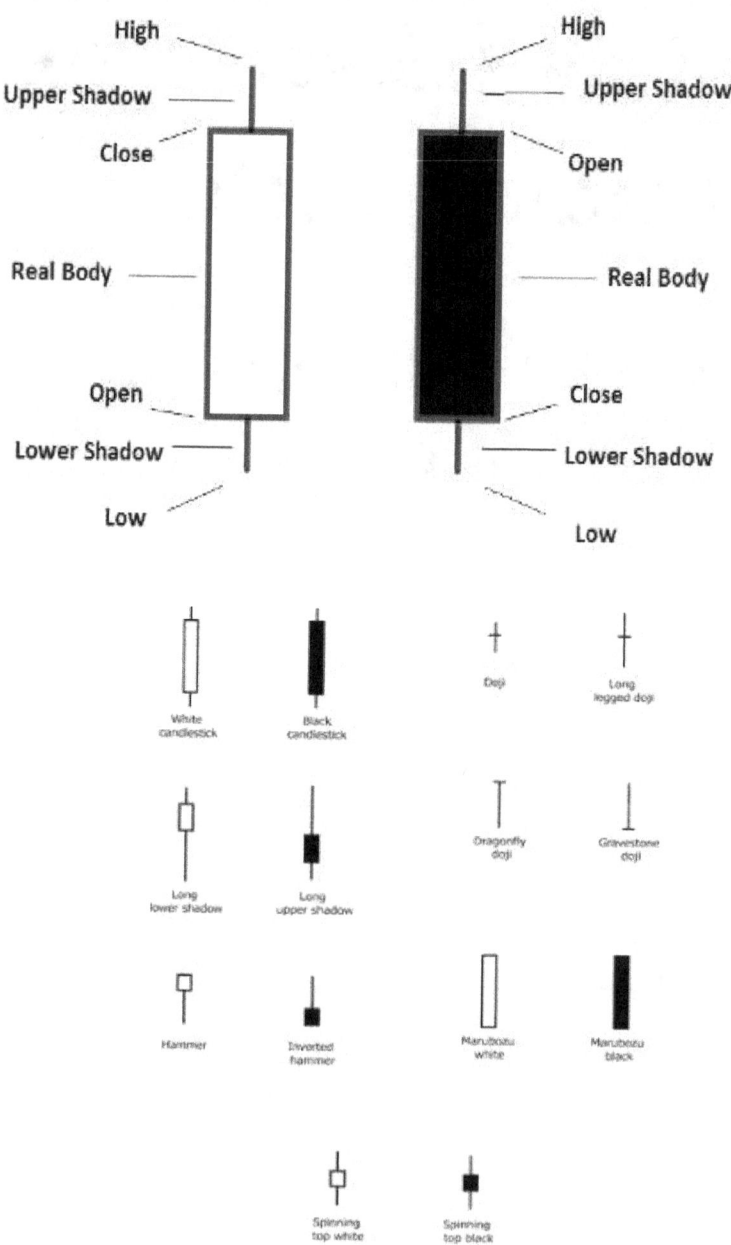

A doji is a tug-of-war in which neither the bulls nor the bears are winning. It represents an equilibrium between supply and demand. Since prices have risen in an uptrend, the bulls have, by definition, won previous battles. The most recent skirmish's outcome is now in doubt. The opposite holds true after a prolonged downtrend. Prices have fallen as a result of the bears' previous victories. The bulls may be ready to turn the tide now that they have the fortitude to buy.

For example = INET

Doji Star

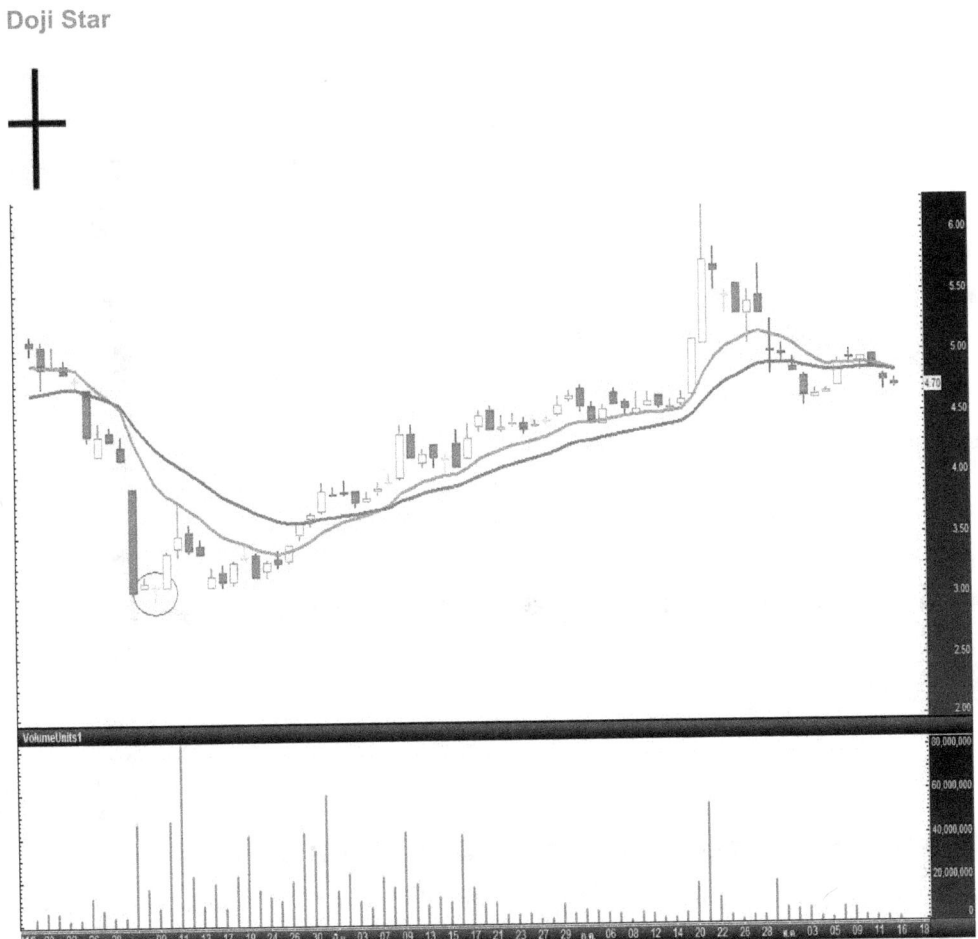

A candle with "long legs" is much more dramatic. It states that prices rose significantly throughout the day before profit taking took over. Typically, a significant upper shadow remains. A nearby beneath the midpoint of the flame shows a ton of shortcoming. Here is an illustration of a doji with long legs.

For example = K

Long-legged Doji

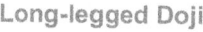

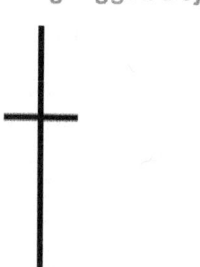

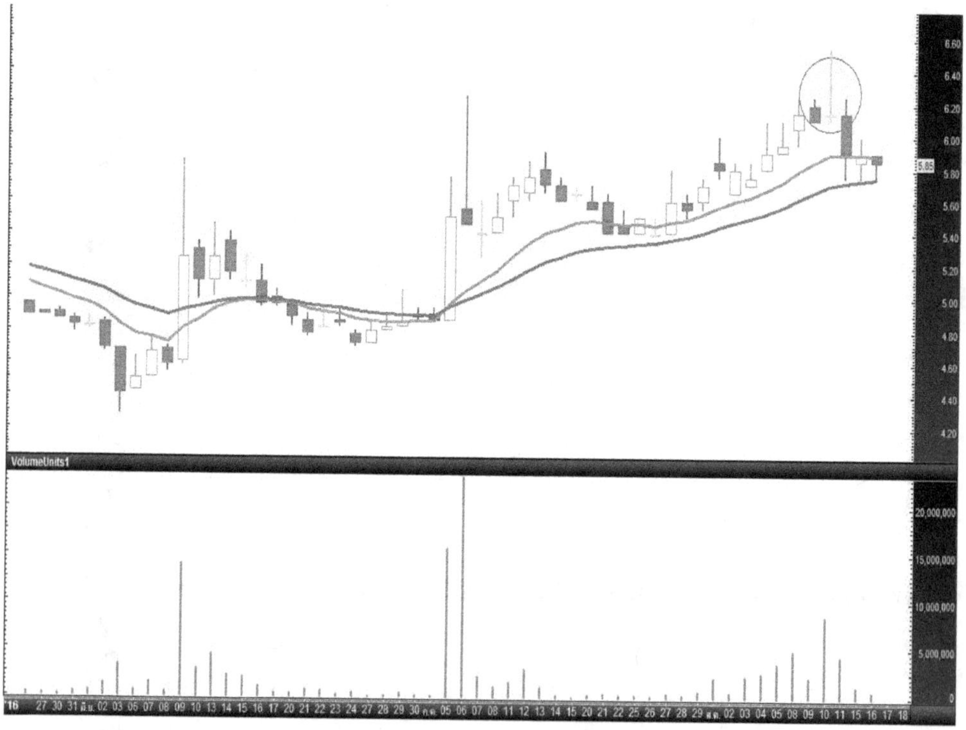

A "gravestone doji," as the name suggests, is probably the most ominous candle of all. On that particular day, price rallied, but it was too much for them to handle. When the day is over. When they returned, they closed on the same level. A gravestone doji can look something like this:

Gravestone Doji

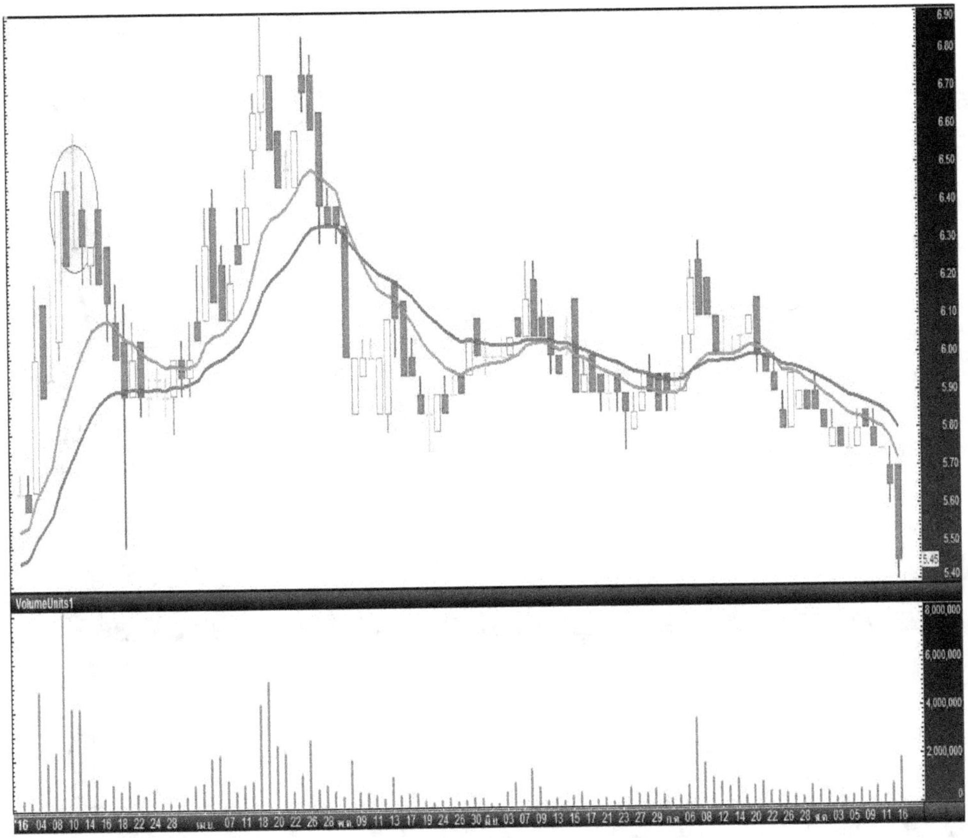

A "Dragonfly" doji depicts a day when prices rose, fell, and then returned to their initial levels. Dragonflies aren't very common. However, if the stock is not already overbought as demonstrated by Bollinger bands and indicators like stochastic, when they do occur, they frequently resolve positively.

For example = DSGT

Dragonfly Doji

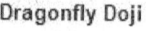

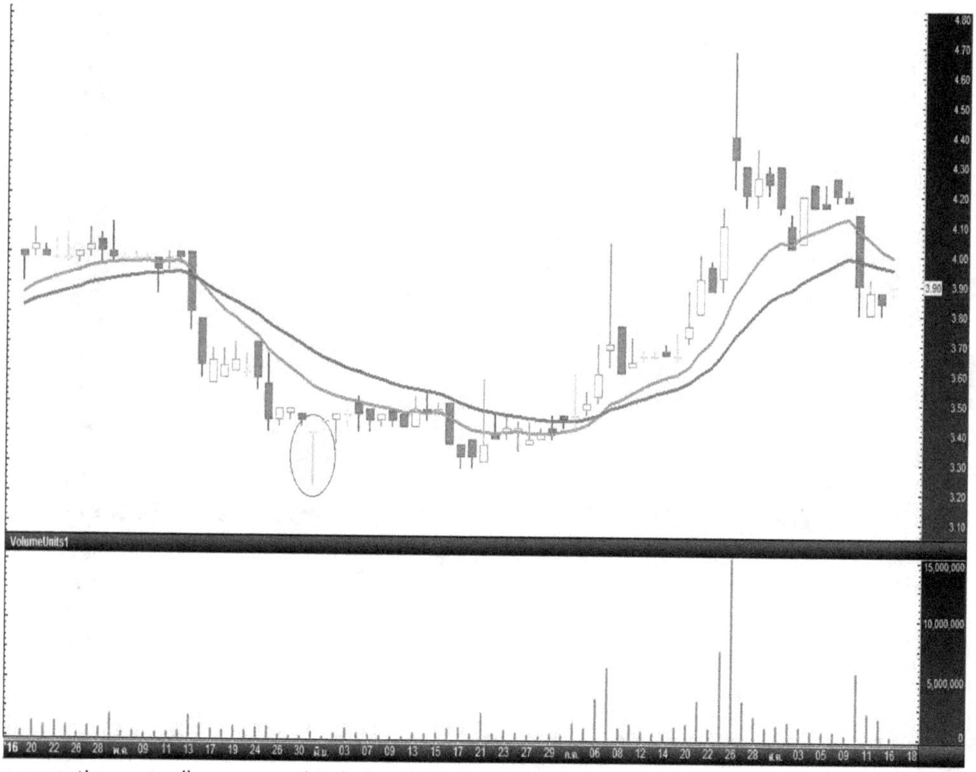

The executioner candle, so named in light of the fact that it seems to be an individual who has been executed with legs swinging underneath, consistently happens after a drawn out upturn The executioner happens on the grounds that dealers, seeing an auction in the offers, rush in to snatch the stock a deal cost.

The Hanging Man signal cannot be valid unless the following conditions are met:

• Prior to this signal, the stock must have been in a distinct uptrend. This can be outwardly seen on the outline.

• The size of the lower shadow must at least double that of the body.

- There should be continued sales the day after the Hanging Man is formed.

- There ought to be no or very little upper shadow. It doesn't matter what color the body is, but a black body would be better than a white body.

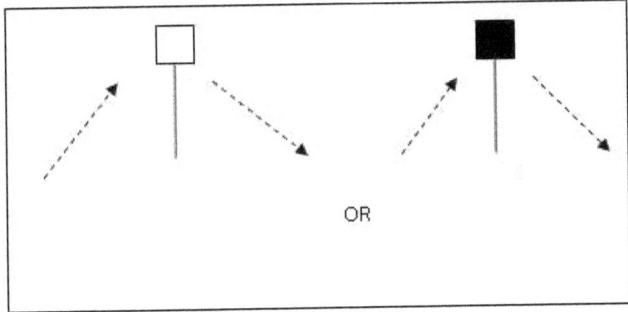

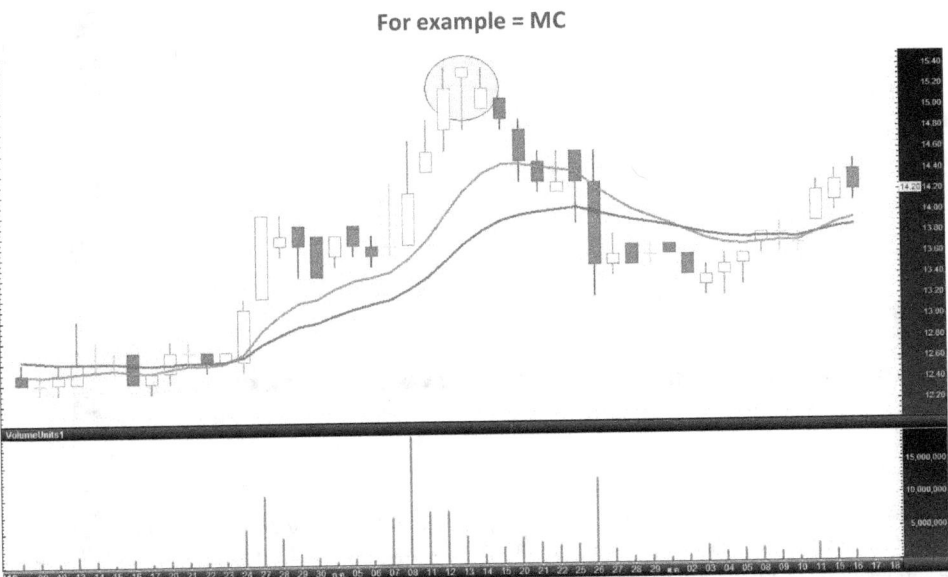

For example = MC

After a prolonged downtrend, the hammer shows up. Strong selling typically begins at the opening bell on the day of the hammer candle. However, the market recovers throughout the day and closes close to or even higher than the previous day's high. The market may be "hammering" out a bottom in these instances.

The Hammer signal cannot be valid unless the following conditions are met:

- Prior to this signal, the stock must have been in a distinct downtrend. On the chart, you can see this clearly.

- The size of the lower shadow must at least double that of the body.

- On the day that the Hammer is formed, one ought to observe continued purchases.

- There ought to be no or very little upper shadow. It doesn't matter what color the body is, but a white body would be better than a black body.

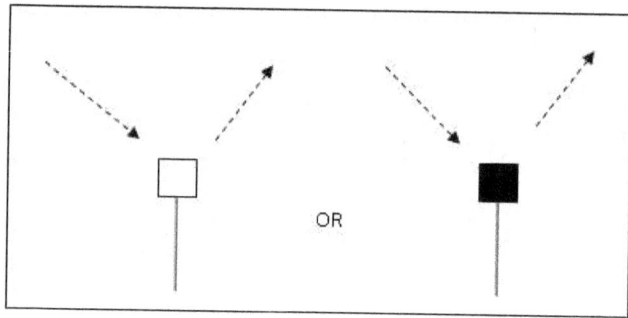

For example = KCE

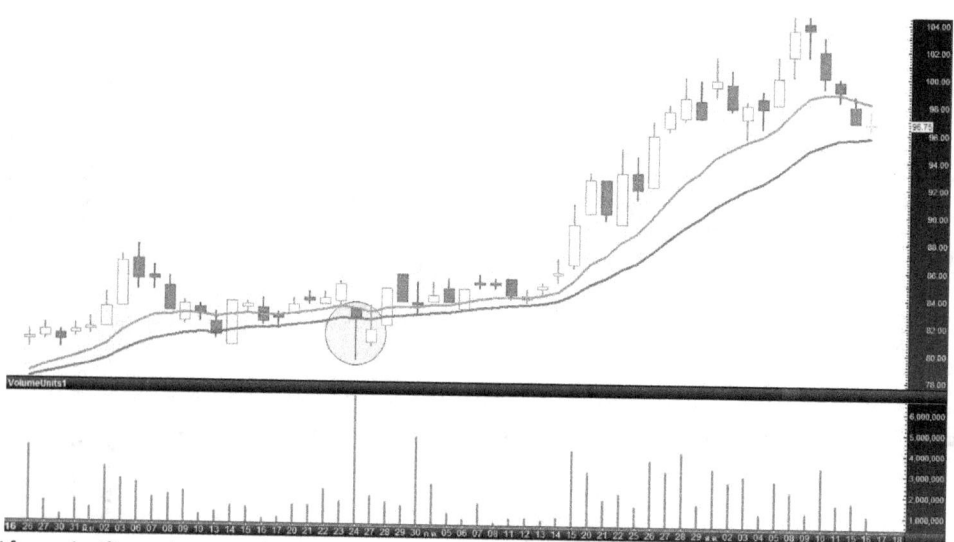

After a significant downtrend, a bullish engulfing candle appears. It is important to keep in mind that the engulfing candle must surround the shadow but not the actual body of the previous candle.

The following conditions must be met for the Bullish Engulfing signal to be valid:

- Prior to this signal, the stock must have been in a distinct downtrend. On the chart, you can see this clearly.
- A white candle should open below the previous day's Close and close above the previous day's black candle Open on the second day of the signal.

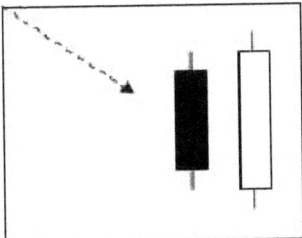

For example = MINT

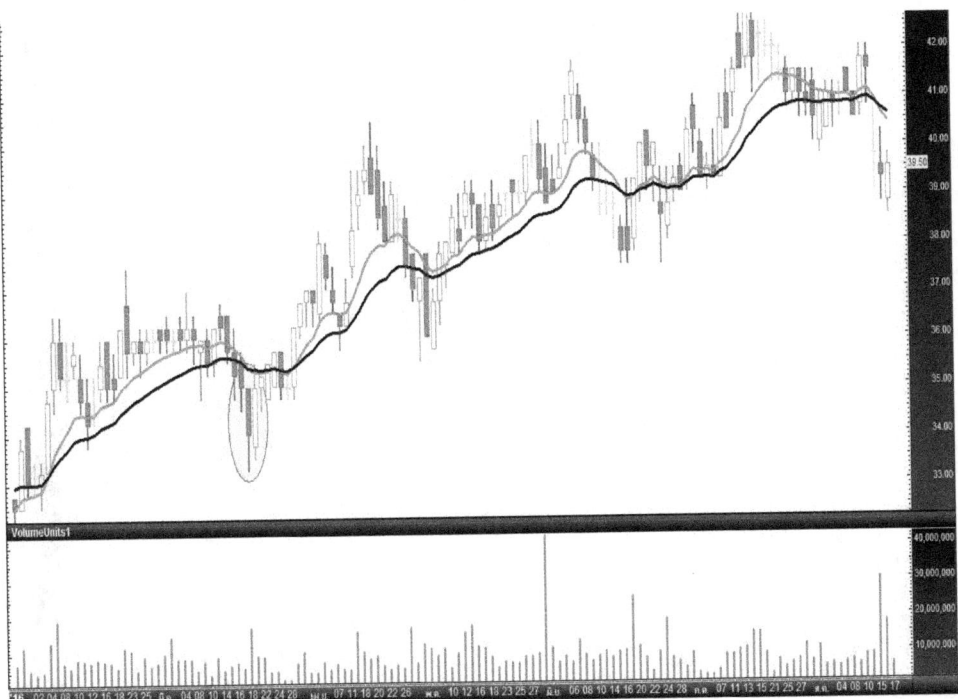

After a significant uptrend, a bearish engulfing candle occurs. Again, there is no need to surround the shadows.

The following conditions must be met for the Bullish Engulfing signal to be valid:

- Prior to this signal, the stock must have been in a distinct downtrend. On the chart, you can see this clearly.
- A white candle should open below the previous day's Close and close above the previous day's Black Candle Open on the second day of the signal.

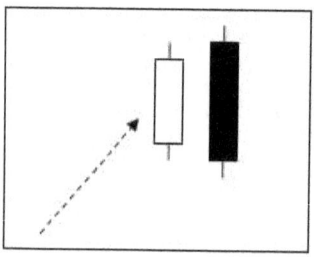

For example = ECL

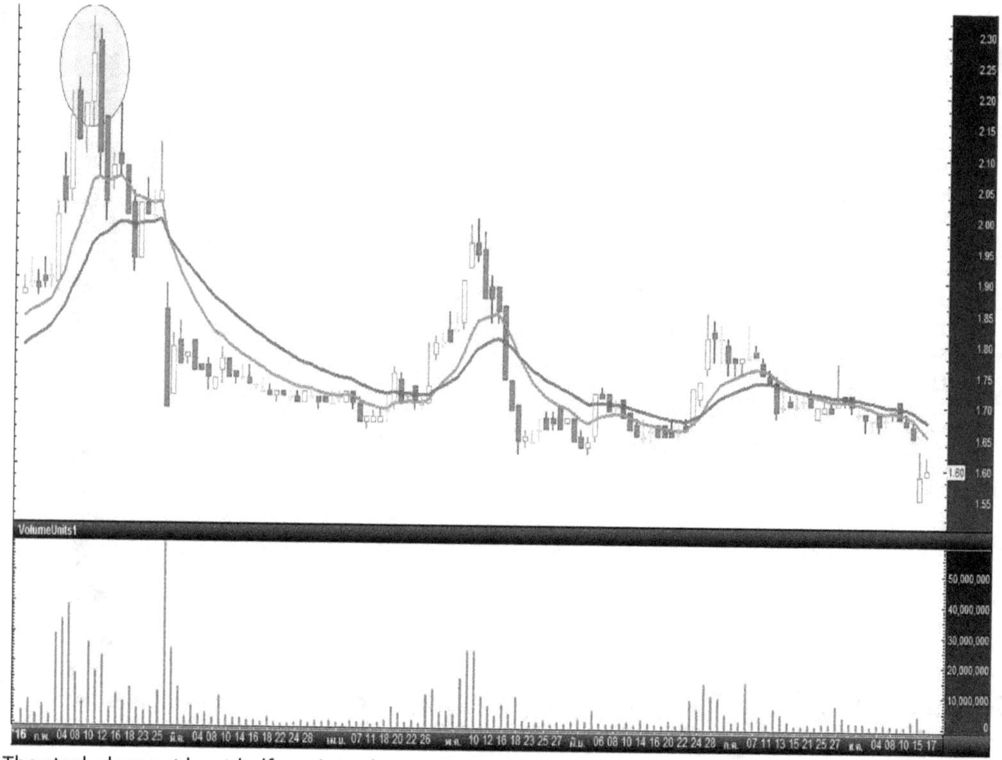

The stock closes at least halfway into the previous white capping candle on the day of dark cloud cover. The signal is stronger the larger the previous candle's penetration, or how close this candle is to being a bearish engulfing. If a dark cloud cover candle occurs at a significant resistance area and if there is a lot of volume at the end of the day, traders should pay close attention to it.

The following conditions must be met for the Dark Cloud signal to be valid:

- Prior to this signal, the stock must have been in a distinct uptrend. On the chart, you can see this clearly.
- A black candle should open above the previous day's high and close more than half way into the white candle's body on the second day of the signal.

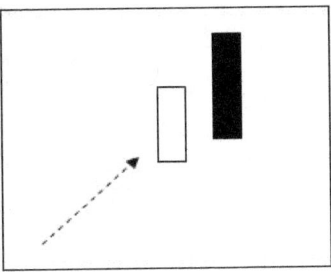

For example = SCN

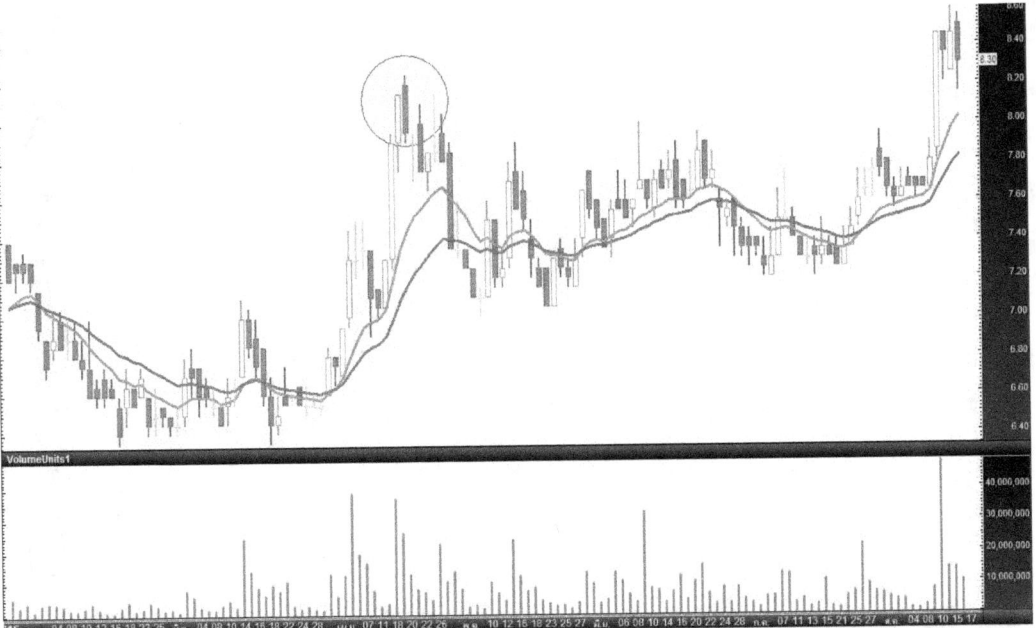

The day before the piercing candle appears, the daily candle should ideally have a fairly large dark real body, indicating a strong down day. The piercing pattern frequently will end a minor downtrend (a downtrend that typically lasts between five and fifteen trading days). The classic piercing pattern features a gap between the next day's candle and the lower shadow, or low, from the previous day.

For the Penetrating sign to be substantial, the accompanying circumstances should exist:

- Prior to this signal, the stock must have been in a distinct downtrend. This can be outwardly seen on the outline.
- A white candle should open below the previous day's low and close more than half way into the body of the previous day's black candle on the second day of the signal.

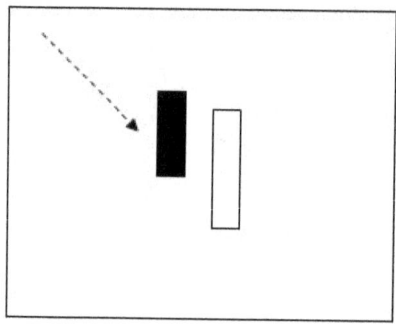

For example = SET INDEX

During a long-term uptrend, the evening star pattern appears. We observe a candle with a long, white body on the first day. The bulls appear to have full control of the stock, and everything appears to be normal. However, on the second day, a star candle appears. The stock must gap higher on the day of the star in order for this to be a valid evening star pattern. The star can be white or black. A star candle typically has a large upper shadow and a small real body. A candle with a black real body appears on the third day. This candle sinks significantly into the first day's actual body. If there is a gap between the candles on the second and third days, the pattern becomes more powerful. However, especially when it comes to equity trading, this gap is unusual. The reversal signal becomes more potent the further this third candle moves back into the actual body of the first day's candle.

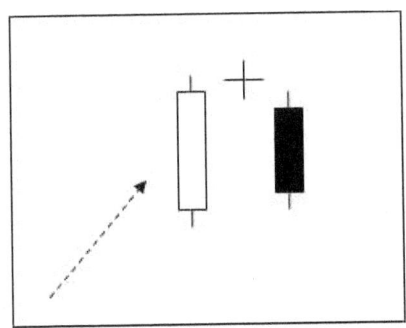

For example = TRUE

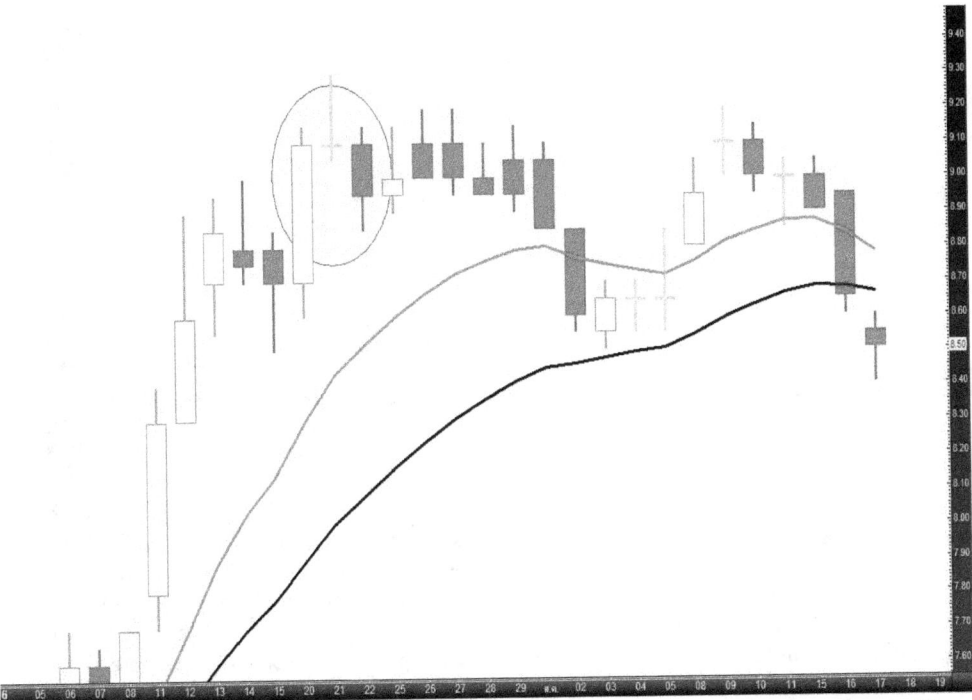

The morning star, which appears like a large, dark candle on the first day. Despite having a small lower shadow, the upper shadow on top of a small real body gives the middle day star its star quality. The reversal is completed by a large white candle in the third candle. Not in the way that the third candle recovered nearly to the first-day highs and occurred on high volume.

The following conditions must be met for the Morning Star signal to be valid:

- Prior to this signal, the stock must have been in a distinct downtrend. This can be outwardly seen on the graph.

- A long, dark body must appear on the first day of the signal. It must be a day of uncertainty on the second day. The long white candle on the third day ought to extend at least halfway into the body of the dark candle on the first day..

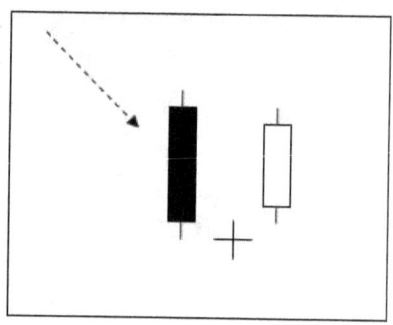

For example = VIBHA

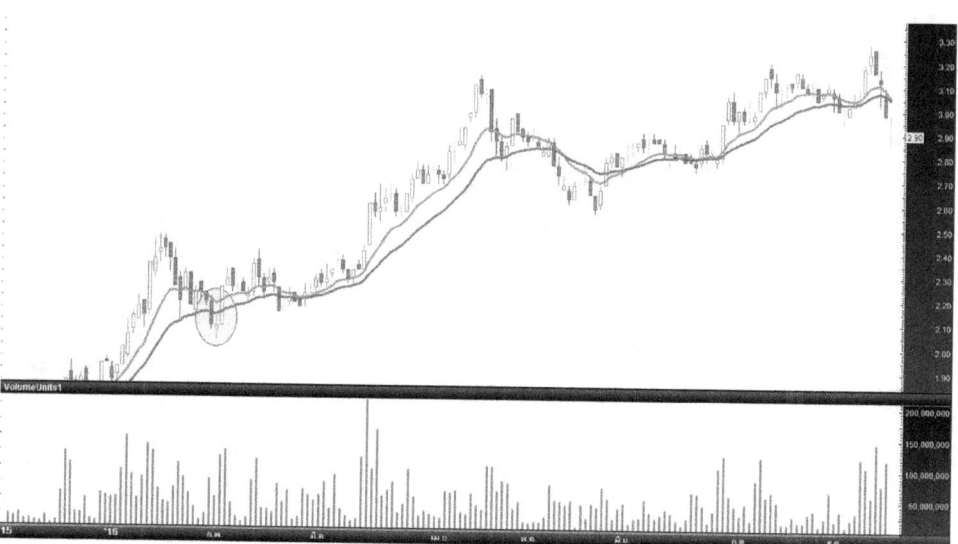

The shooting star can only appear at a potential peak in the market. When a candle with a large real body follows a shooting star, it typically serves as a much stronger warning because it demonstrates that the price cannot maintain high levels. The day the meteorite happens, the market in a perfect world ought to hole higher. The stock ought to then surge significantly. The longs appear to be completely in charge at this point. Profit taking, on the other hand, occurs sometime during the day. A small real body demonstrates that the stock closes close to the market's unchanged level. As a result, a shooting star has a large upper shadow and a small real body. Usually, there won't be a lower shadow or it won't be very big.

The Shooting Star signal is valid only if the following conditions are met:

- Prior to this signal, the stock must have been in a distinct uptrend. On the chart, you can see this clearly.
- The upper shadow needs to be at least twice as big as the person in it.
- Sales should continue the following day after the Shooting Star is formed.
- There ought to be no or very little lower shadow. It doesn't matter what color the body is; a black

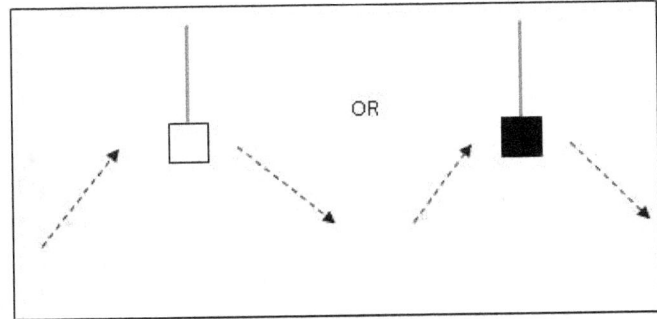

For example = WICE

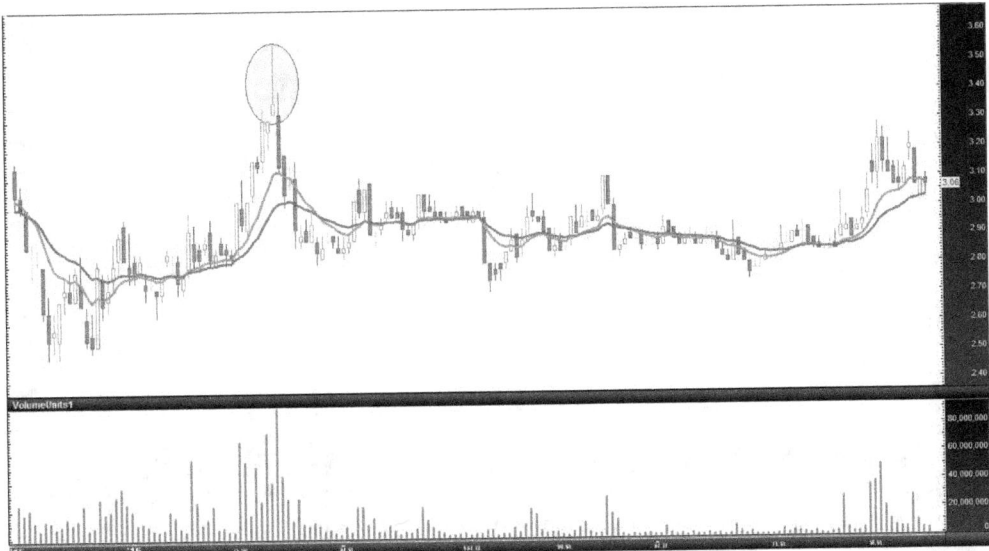

Since the stock is probably already oversold, the inverted hammer can only occur after a prolonged downtrend. Therefore, the inverted hammer indicates that traders with long positions in the security, the majority of whom are currently suffering significant losses, frequently sell into strength to dump their shares quickly.

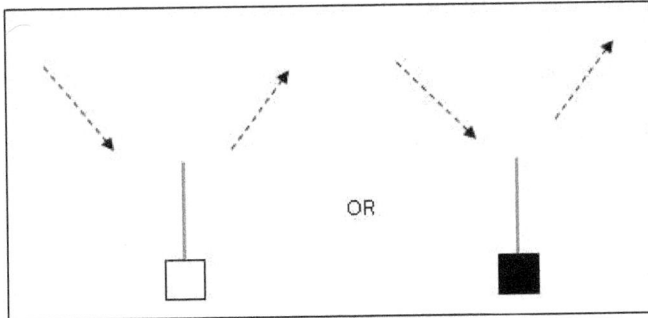

For example = STEC

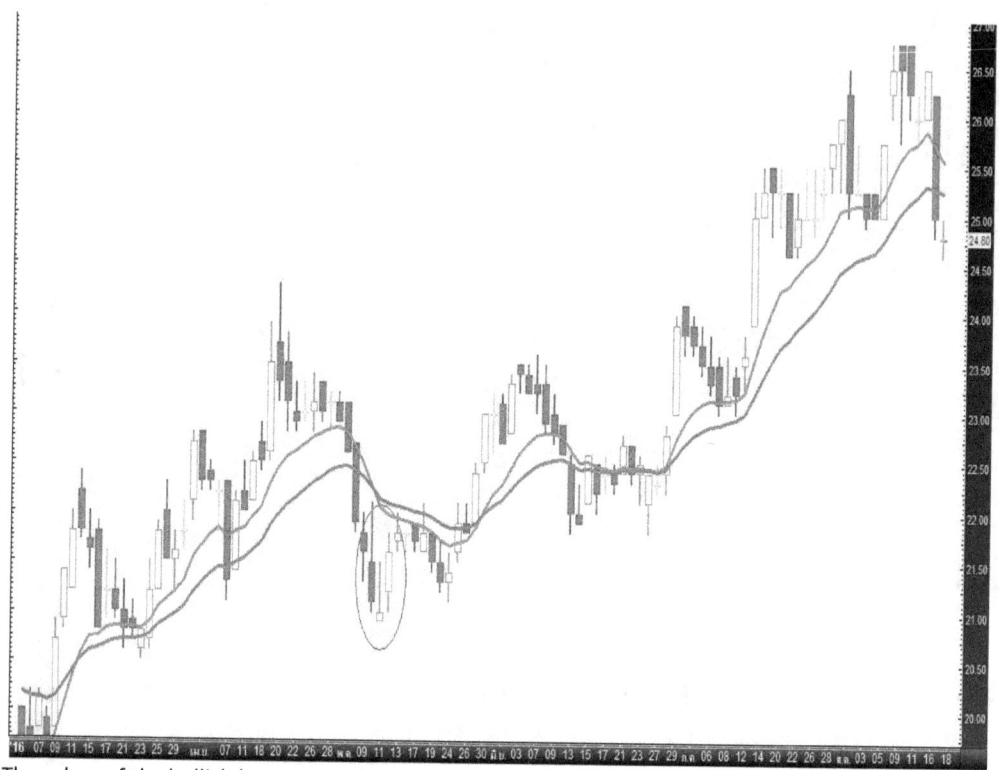

The colors of the bullish harami candle are reversed, so it can occur in either a bearish or bullish trend: A bullish signal is given when a larger black body moves ahead of a smaller white real body: It suggests that the stock is on the verge of rising. In signal: The upper and lower shadows of a bullish or bearish harami can be of any size, and theoretically they could even go above the actual body of the clear candle day. However, in practice, the harami day's shadows are typically quite small and well contained within the actual body of the candle from the previous day.

The following conditions must be met for the Bullish Harami signal to be valid:

- Prior to this signal, the stock must have been in a distinct downtrend. On the chart, you can see this clearly.
- A white candle should open above the previous day's Close and close below the previous day's Black Candle Open on the second day of the signal.

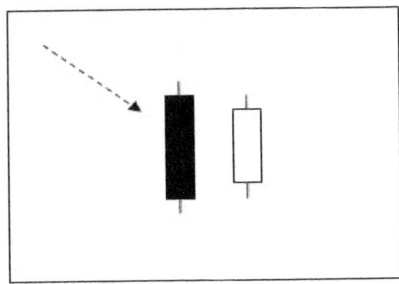

For example = CPF

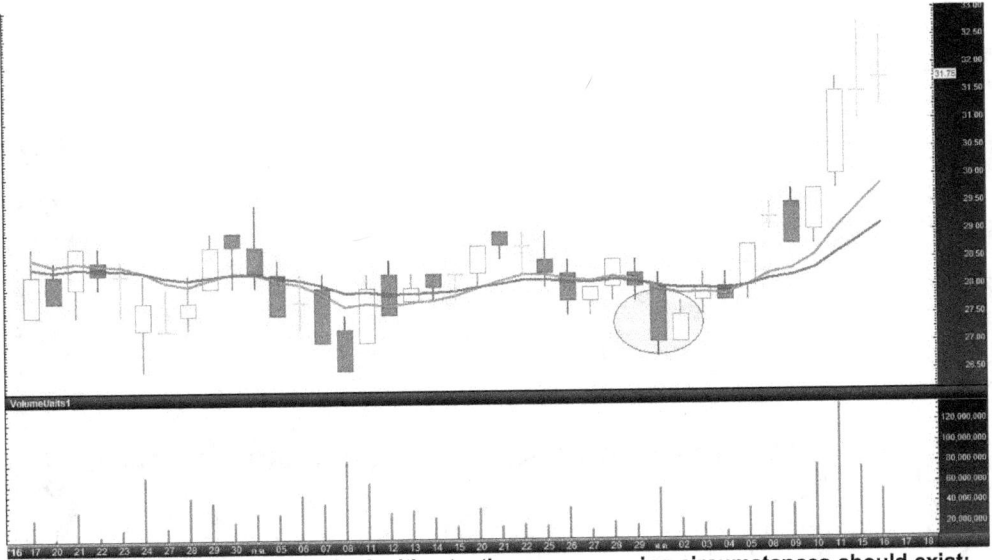

For the Negative Harami sign to be legitimate, the accompanying circumstances should exist:

- Prior to this signal, the stock must have been in a distinct uptrend. On the chart, you can see this clearly.
- A dark candle should open below the previous day's Close and close above the previous day's White Candle Open on the second day of the signal.

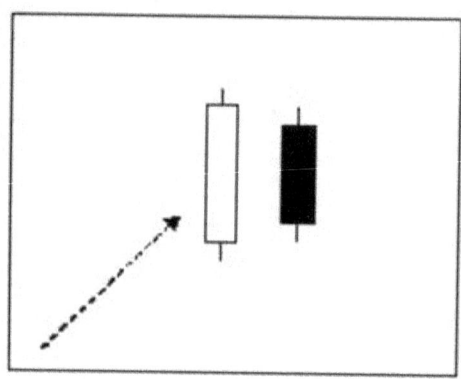

For example = BBL

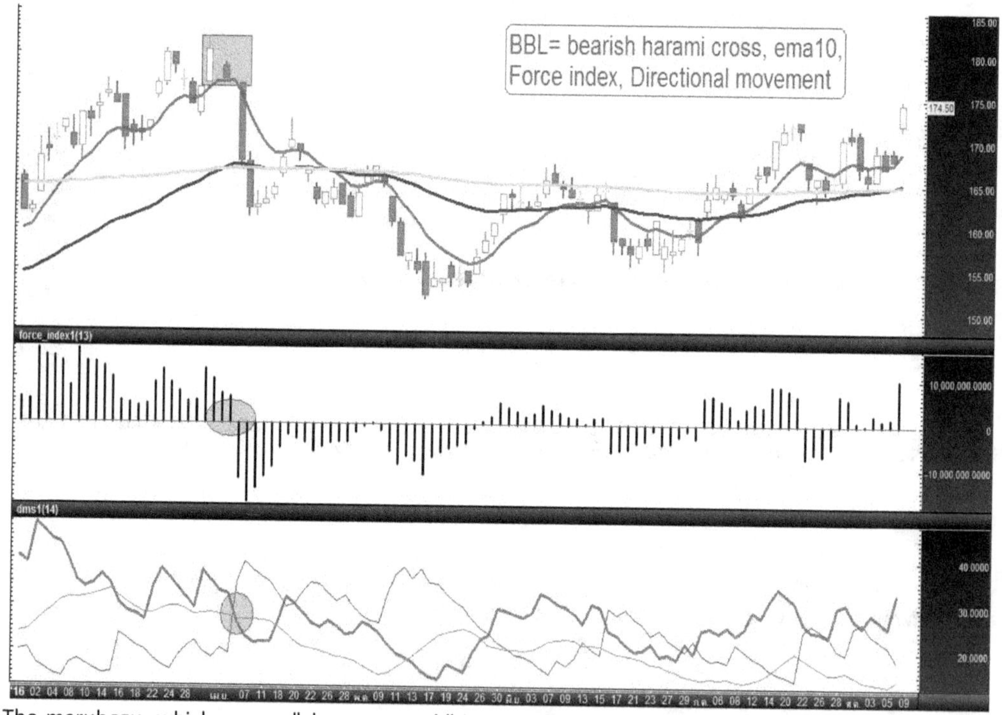

BBL= bearish harami cross, ema10, Force index, Directional movement
force_index1(13)
dms1(14)

The marubozu, which means "close-cropped," is typically a long candle that indicates a wide trading range for the day. There is neither an upper nor a lower shadow on a marubozu candle. Rarely, it may not have either an upper or lower shadow. It's important to note when a marubozu is full or very close to being full. If it's a white candle, buyers will be extremely persuaded. On the other hand, a dark candle indicates that the sellers were eager to leave. As always, you should pay close attention to the trading on the next day to see if there is any continuation. A full or almost full marubozu suggests that there is solid trading interest contingent upon the variety. The stock is likely to continue trending in the same direction for the following few sessions if there is follow through early the following day. The trader may benefit from this awareness.

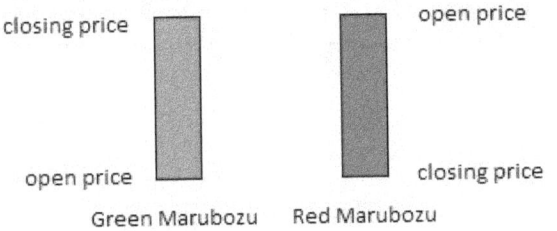

For example = INTUCH

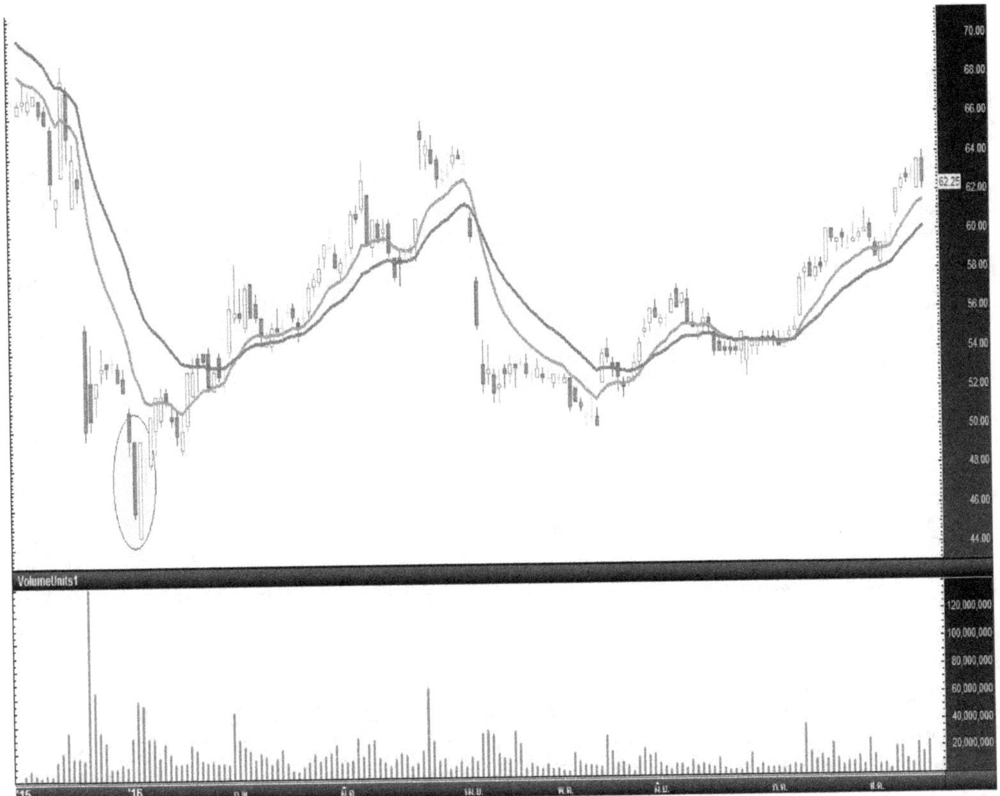

Spin top, the candle has a very limited range, and the shadows are relatively small. When low volume is combined, traders may be showing that they are not interested.

High-Wave Spinning Top Definition:

A spinning top wave candle, also known as a high wave candle, is a candlestick whose open and close prices are close to one another. This results in a small real body and the color has no effect. Additionally, their upper and lower shadows are significantly longer than their body length. Candlesticks of this kind signify uncertainty and then consolidation.

Use in Real Life:

Technical analysts frequently "join the sidelines" when they spot spinning top high wave candlesticks. Traders will frequently wait for additional confirmation of an upward or downward price movement after such a volatile session.

Spinning Top High Wave

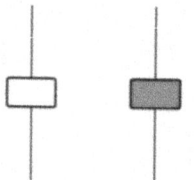

For example = SET INDEX

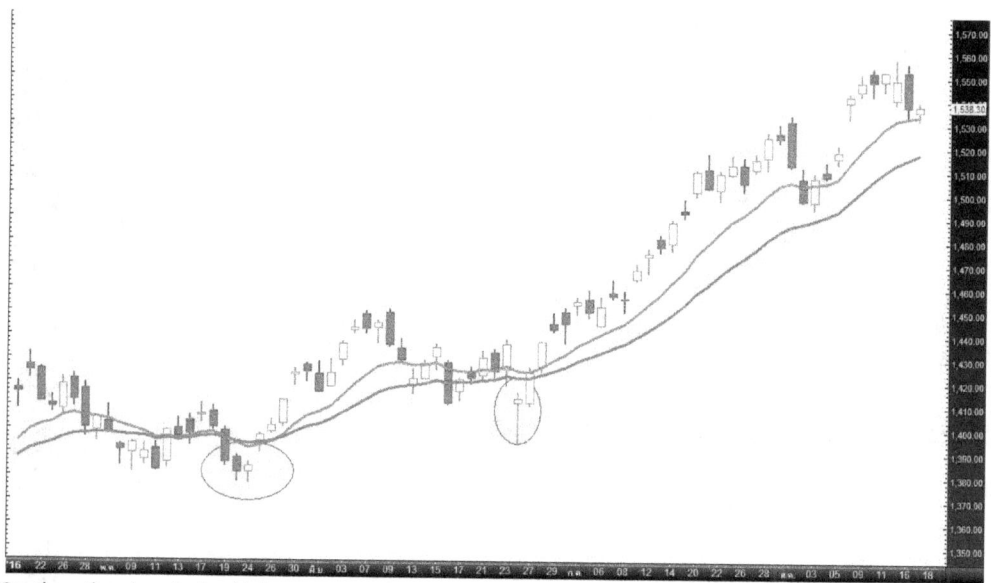

On the other hand, the high wave candle depicts a situation in which the bulls and bears are actively engaged in a tug-of-war. The market has lost its clear sense of direction, as evidenced by this candle. If it occurs on a large scale, it indicates that the market as a whole is unsure of where prices are headed.

- High Wave candles show the confusion among traders
- The actual body's size demonstrates that traders do not agree on how to maintain the current trend.
- Predicts a possible change in the current uptrend or downtrend.
- There is a tiny real body in either color on the candle.
- The size of the two shadows are especially lengthy, however are not expected to be precisely the same length
- Avoid trading within a range: The price is holding before rising.
- Candles of this kind should be handled with care.

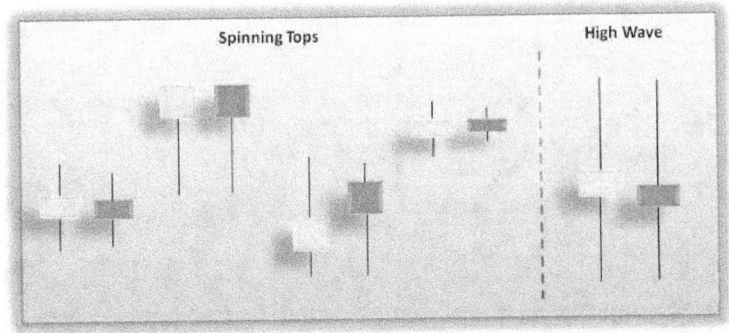

Swing traders should pay close attention to the crow's caw when stock traders encounter the three black crows candle formation. The candlestick is represented by three crows perched atop a tall tree. If the first "crow" or dim candle closes beneath the previous light's actual body on the day the first dark crow appears, the development is typically foreshadowed. After that, there are two more long, down days. The stock opens higher than the earlier day's nearby on every one of nowadays, giving its desired impression to recapture its past strength. However, the stock reaches a new closing low as the sellers regain control at the conclusion of each session.

THREE CROWS / LPN

The three white soldiers pattern is most potent when it occurs following a prolonged period of consolidation and decline. When a stock shows sideways movement after a decline, the appearance of three white soldiers indicates that higher prices are likely to follow. A reversal candle is the first of the three white soldiers. It either signals the end of a downtrend or that the stock is emerging from a consolidation phase following a decline. The candle on day two might ignite during the first day's actual body. As long as the second candle opens in the upper half of day one's range, the pattern is valid. The stock should close to its high on day two, leaving only a very small or nonexistent upper shadow. On day three, the same pattern is repeated.

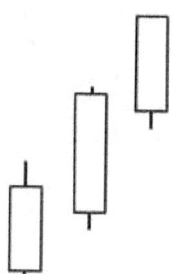

For example = BEM

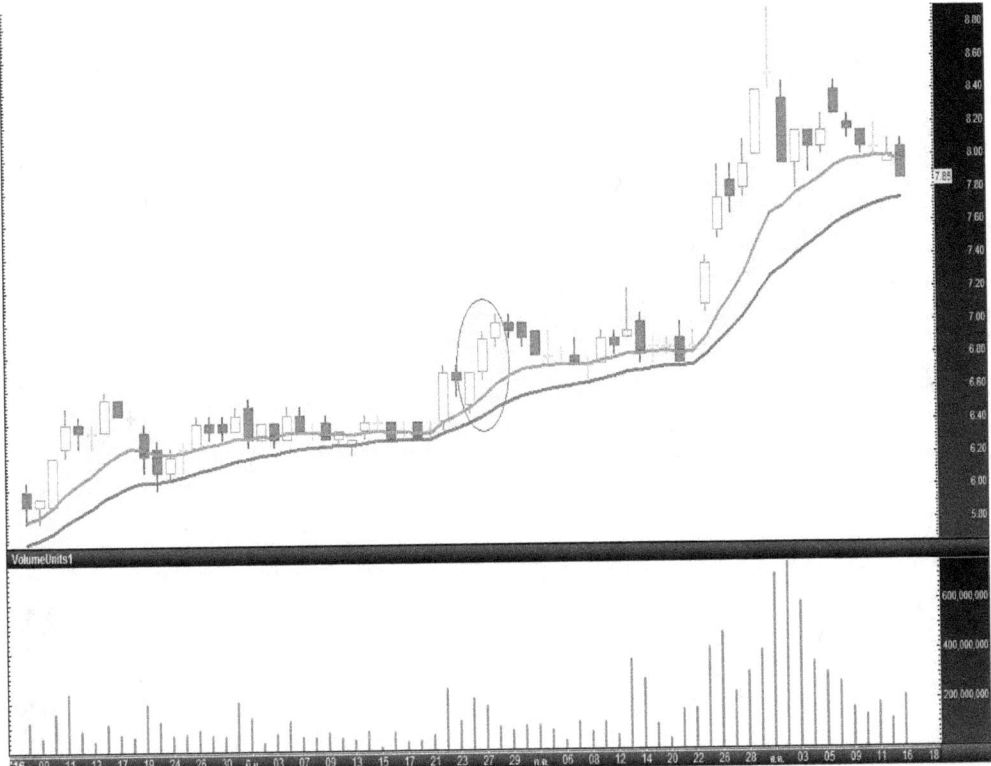

There are always two candles involved in the tweezers formation. The high cost of two nearby sessions is nearly identical at a tweezers top. In an expensive stock there might be a couple of pennies variety, and I devotee it ought to in any case be viewed as a tweezers. The lowest price for two sessions that occur simultaneously at a tweezers bottom is the same. Let's just talk about the bottom of the tweezers for simplicity's sake. Sometimes, the bottom of the tweezers is made up of two real candlestick bodies that have the same low. In other instances, the stock bounces higher when the lower shadows of two nearby candles touch the same price level. A third possibility is that the bottom level of the lower shadow from one day and the real body from a nearby session meet.

Tweezers

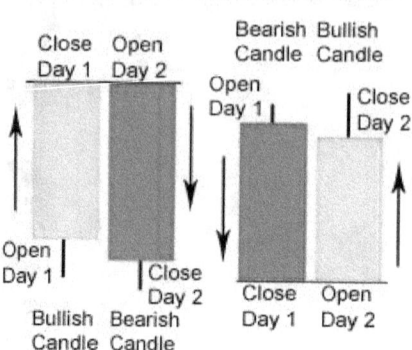

For example = BH

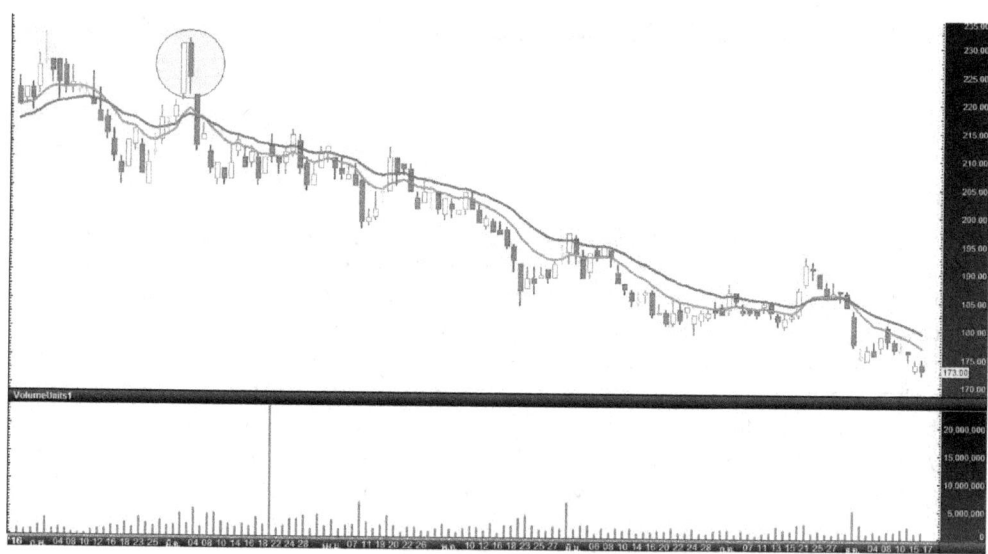

For example = STEC

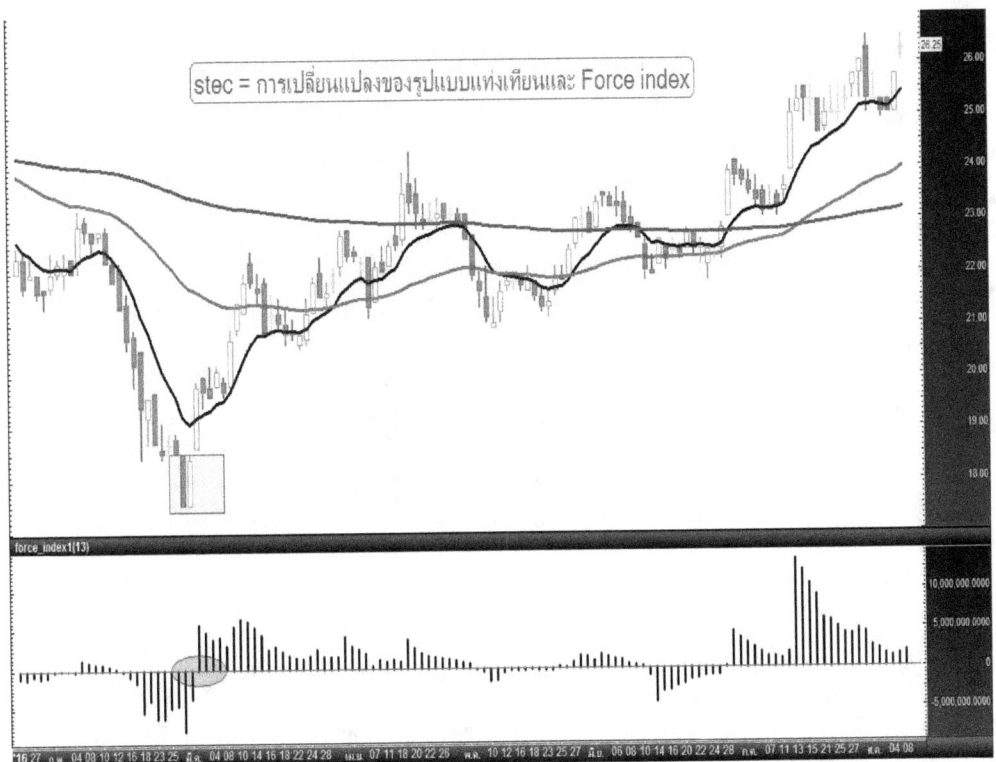

Stick Sandwich

During a Downtrend, it occurs; The candles that follow the Pattern require confirmation. The First Candle is black and has a brief Lower shadow—or it does not have a Lower shadow at all—that indicates a new low in the downtrend.

— The white Second Candle has the Open above the First Candle's Close (the Real Body is above the First Candle's Close).

— The black Third Candle has an Open that is higher than the Second Candle's Close, while the Close is at or near the same level as the First Candle's Close (in order to fully contain the Real Body of the Second Candle).

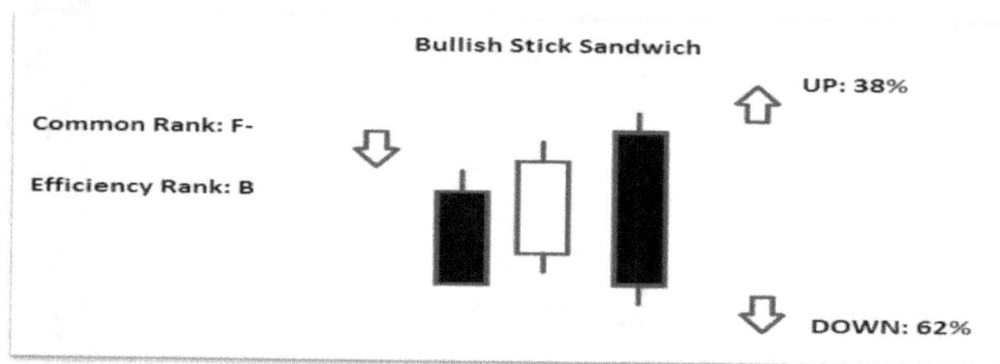

During an Uptrend, it occurs; Candles that adhere to the Pattern necessitate confirmation.
The first candle, which is white and does not have an upper shadow at all, is a new high in the uptrend.
The Subsequent Candle is dark, it has the Nearby underneath the Open of the Primary Flame (The Genuine Body is beneath the End of the Main Light).
The white Third Candle has an Open that is below the Second Candle's Close, but its Close is at or near the same level as the First Candle's Close (in order to fully contain the Second Candle's Real Body).

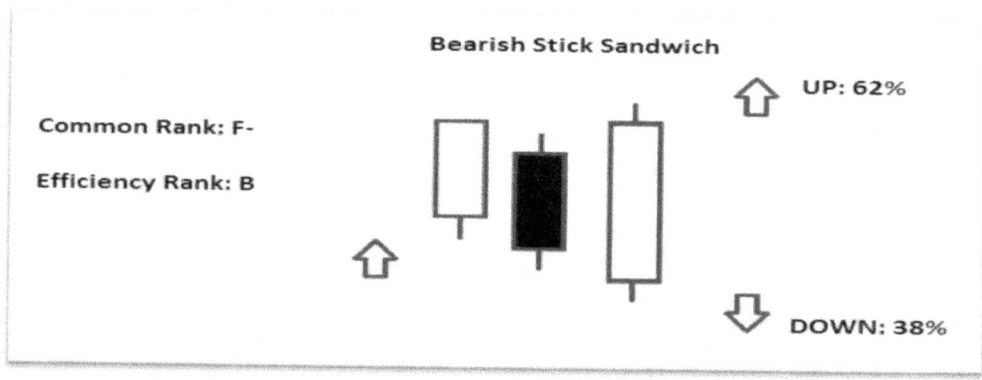

Dumpling top example

In most cases, it should indicate a bearish trend reversal.
— During an Uptrend, it occurs; Candles that adhere to the Pattern necessitate confirmation.
— The pattern begins during an uptrend and transitions into a "Sideways" trend, which symbolizes market uncertainty; There is a trend reversal at the pattern's conclusion, transforming the trend into a downtrend.

– This Pattern is very uncommon; It is crucial that a gap down occurs immediately following the "Sideways" trend and prior to the beginning of the downtrend (in order to obtain additional confirmation of the trend's reversal, as the pattern suggests).

Dumpling Top

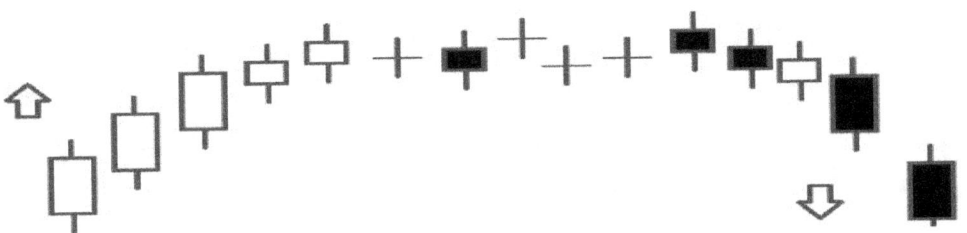

For example = BTS

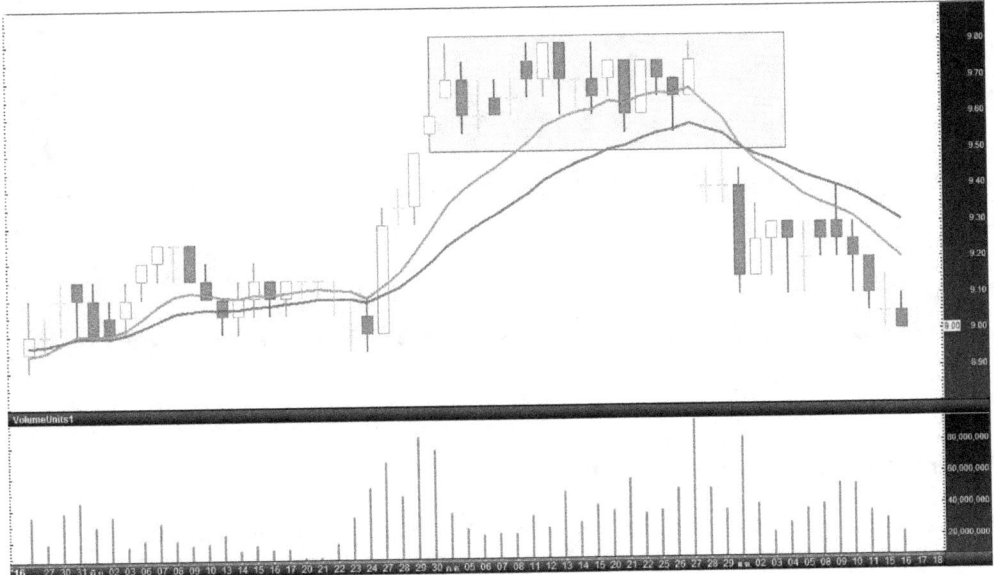

Pattern for fry pan bottom

In most cases, it should indicate a bullish trend reversal.
During a Downtrend, it occurs; affirmation is expected by the candles that follow the Example.
The pattern begins during a downtrend and transitions into a "Sideways" trend, which symbolizes market uncertainty; There is a trend reversal at the pattern's conclusion, transforming the trend into an uptrend.
This Example is very uncommon; It is crucial that there be a gap up immediately following the "Sideways" trend and prior to the beginning of the Uptrend (to obtain additional confirmation of the trend's reversal, as the pattern suggests).

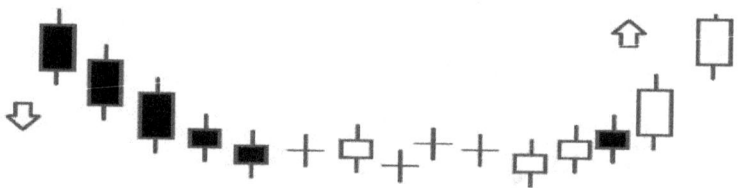

For example = BLA

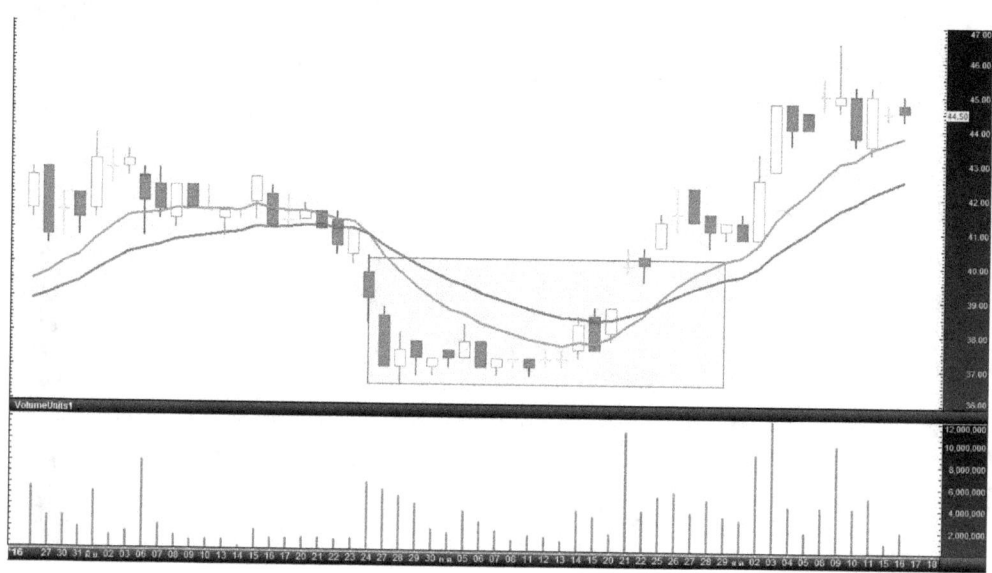

Pattern from the top of the tower

During an Uptrend, it occurs; Candles that adhere to the Pattern necessitate confirmation.
 The Initial Candle is white and long.
 Candles in the "Sideways" phase are spinning tops (black or white) that indicate the market's uncertainty.
 The beginning of the trend's reversal can be seen in the long, black Last Candle.

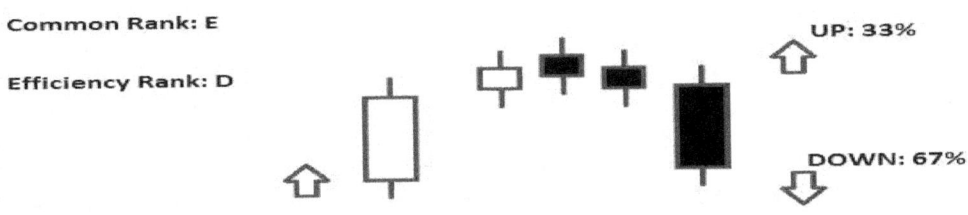

For example = MDX

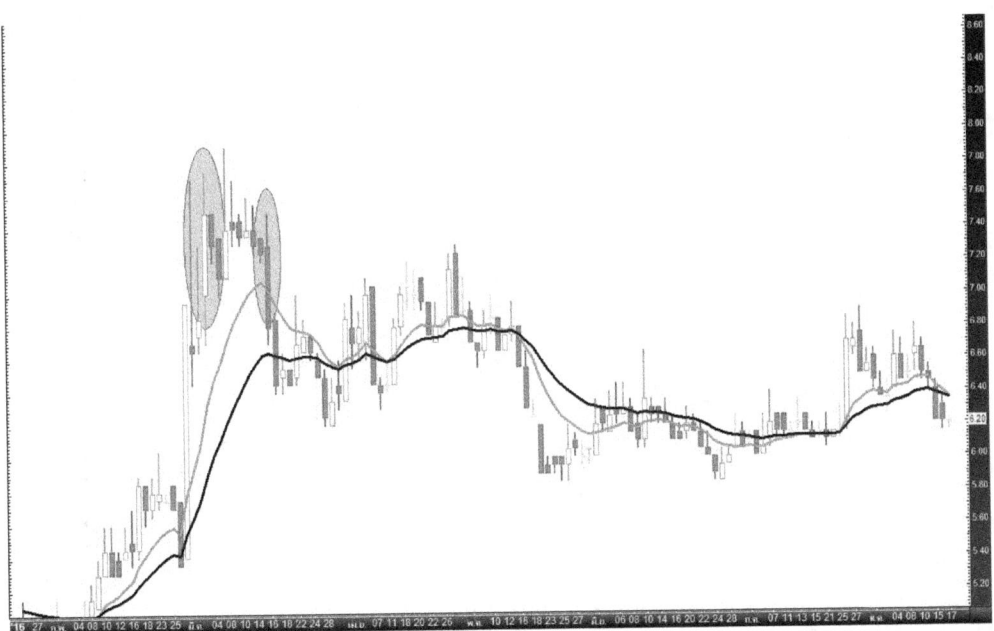

Pattern at the base of the tower

During a Downtrend, it occurs; Candles that adhere to the Pattern necessitate confirmation.
The First Candle is a long, black candle.
The following Candles, which are in the "Sideways" Phase and are spinning tops (black or white), demonstrate the Market's indecisiveness.
The Keep going Candle is long and white, that is the beginning of the inversion of the latest thing.

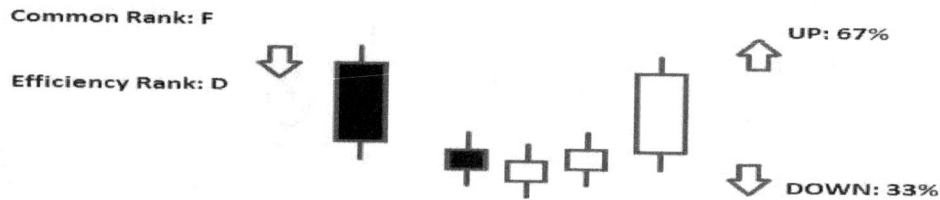

For example = SMPC

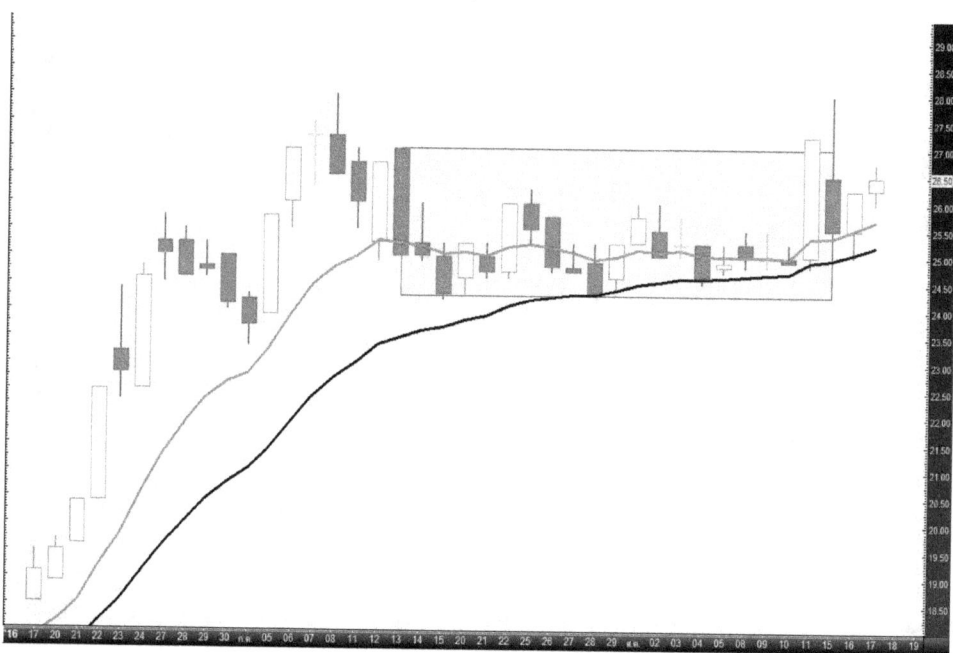

Pattern of Mat Hold

During an Uptrend, it occurs; Candles that adhere to the Pattern necessitate confirmation.
The Initial Candle is white and long.
Between the first and second candles, there is a gap up.
The black Second Candle has a short Real Body; Additionally, the Close is higher than the First Candle's Close.
The Third Candle has a short Real Body and can be white or black—it doesn't matter.
The Fourth Candle has a short Real Body and is black.
The Second, Third and Fourth Flame address a decrease in costs; Additionally, their actual bodies are above the First Candle's low.
The length of the Fifth Candle is white; The Close is higher than the Second Candle's High.

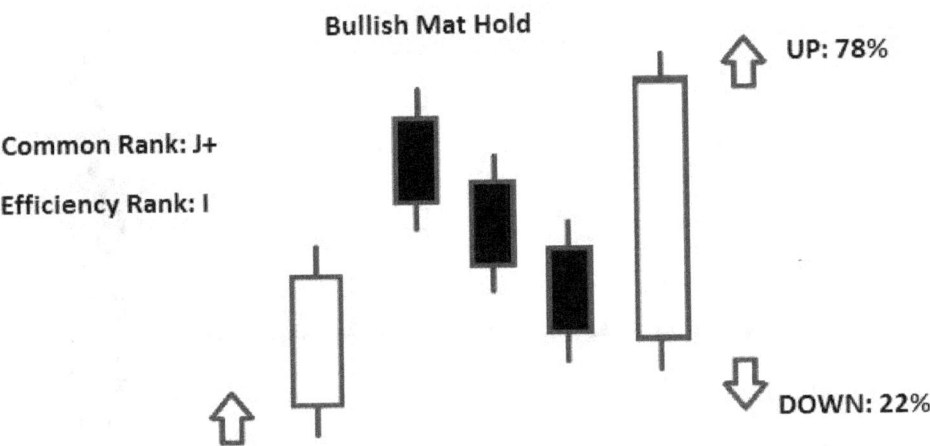

It happens during a Downtrend; Candles that adhere to the Pattern necessitate confirmation.
The First Candle is a long, black candle.
Between the first and second candles, there is a gap down.
The Subsequent Flame is white, it has a short Genuine Body; Additionally, the Close is below the First Candle's Close.
The Third Candle has a short Real Body and can be white or black—it doesn't matter.
The Fourth Candle has a short, white Real Body.
A rise in prices is represented by the Second, Third, and Fourth Candles; Additionally, their actual bodies are below the First Candle's peak.
The length of the Fifth Candle is black; It has a Close that is lower than the Second Candle Low.

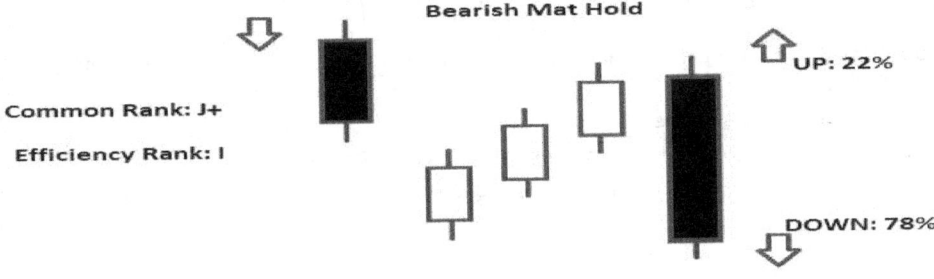

For example = JAS

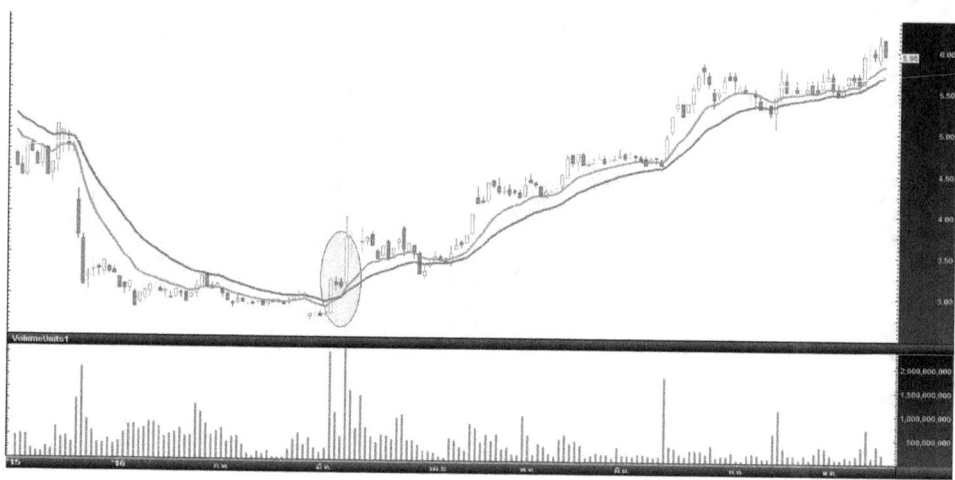

For example = QTC

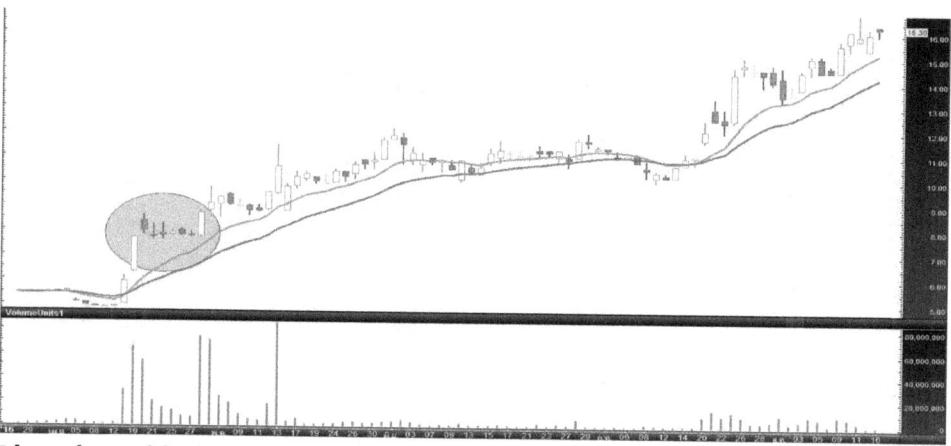

Abandoned baby pattern

During a Downtrend, it occurs; Candles that follow the Pattern do not require confirmation (though it is preferable to look for it).
The First Candle is a long, black candle.
The gap that separates the Second Candle from the First Candle is a Doji candle.
The Third Candle is white, long; The Open is displayed above the Second Candle.

Bullish Abandoned Baby

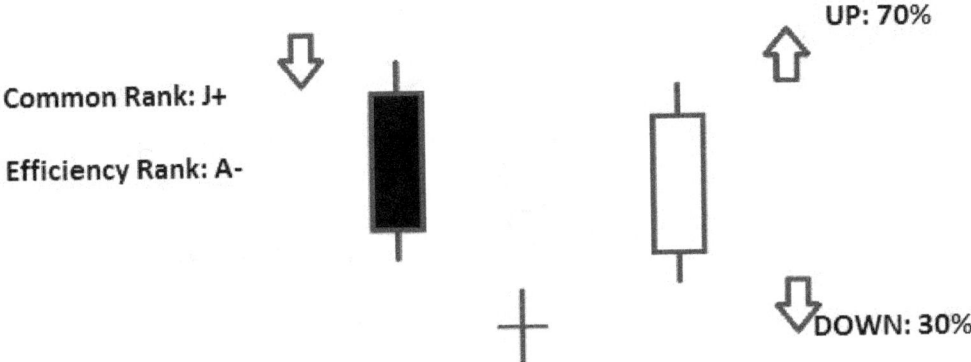

Common Rank: J+

Efficiency Rank: A-

Tri-star doji

During a Downtrend, it occurs; Candles that adhere to the Pattern necessitate confirmation.
– The other two Doji Candles are above the Second Doji..

Bullish Three Star Doji

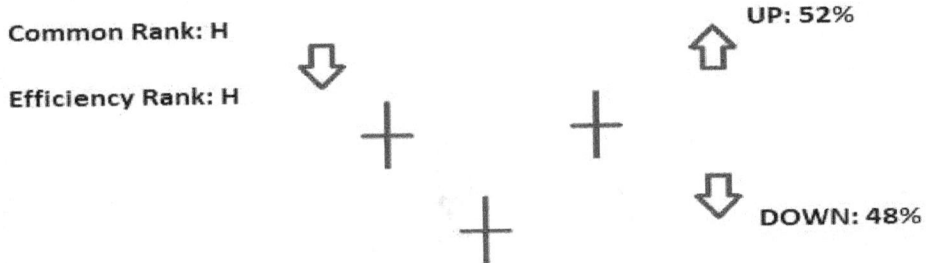

Common Rank: H

Efficiency Rank: H

The stomach pattern is above and below.

Normally, it should indicate a change in the current trend.
It can be found in the variations: Above or Below, depending on which Trend is present.

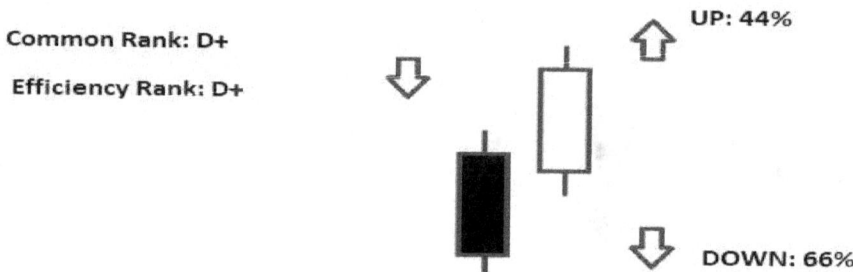

Common Rank: D+
Efficiency Rank: D+

The Stomach Below

During an Uptrend, it occurs; The candles that follow the Pattern require confirmation.
The Initial Candle is white and long.
The Second Candle is black—it could also be white; The Open is either below or at the same level as the Real Body's midpoint in the First Candle. In contrast, the Close is below the First Candle's Open and the First Candle's Real Body's midpoint (in the event that the Second Candle is black).

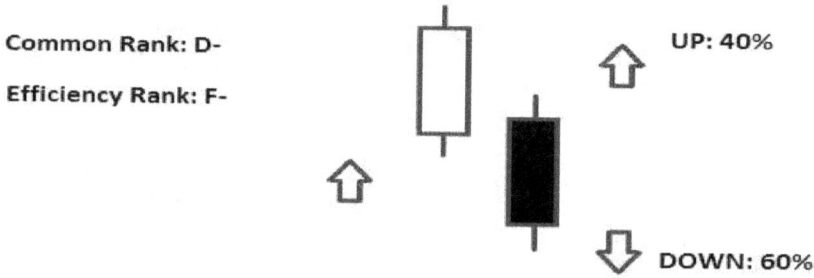

Common Rank: D-
Efficiency Rank: F-

a signal of continuation of the current Trend.

Grabbing Line

Normally it should be
It takes place during an Uptrend or a Downtrend; Candles that adhere to the Pattern necessitate confirmation.
The Pattern is characterized by two candles of opposite hue (in the event of a downtrend, black and white; black and white in the event of an Uptrend).

Common Rank: F

Efficiency Rank: B

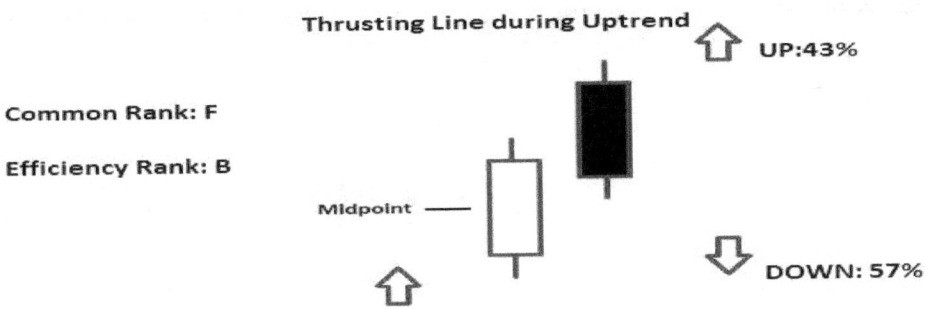

In the event of a downtrend, the first candle is long and black, whereas in the event of an uptrend, it is long and white.
In the event of a downtrend, the Close is close to (but below) the Midpoint of the Real Body of the First Candle, while the Open is below the Low of the First Candle. In the event of an uptrend, the Close is close to (but above) the Midpoint of the Real Body of the First Candle, while the Open is above the High of the First Candle.

a signal of continuation of the current Trend.

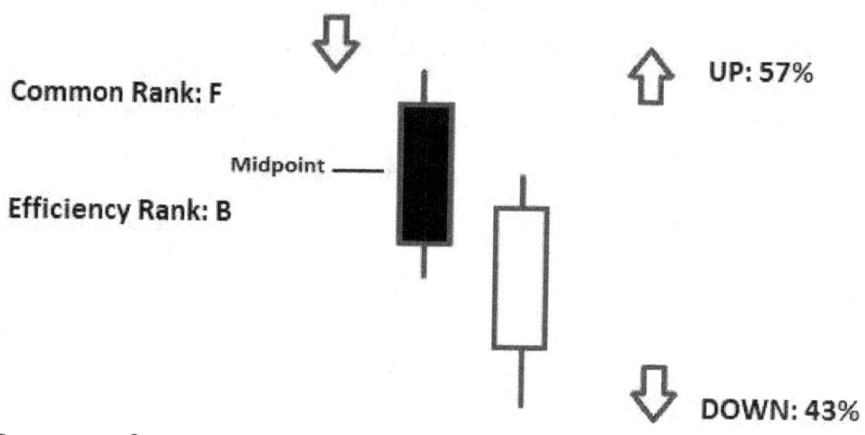

Pattern of separating lines

In most cases, it ought to be
You can find it in the variations: Bearish or bullish, depending on where the Trend is.

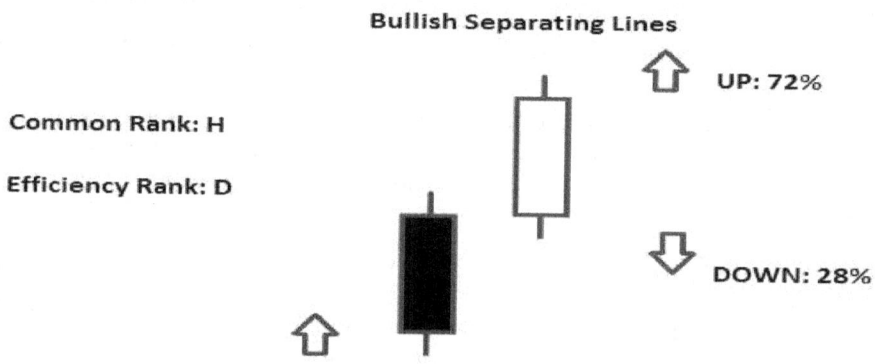

Bearish line of separation

During a Downtrend, it occurs; Candles that adhere to the Pattern necessitate confirmation.
The Initial Candle is white and long.
The Second Candle is a long, black candle; It has the Open at the same level as the First Candle's Open (more or less).

a signal of continuation of the current Trend.

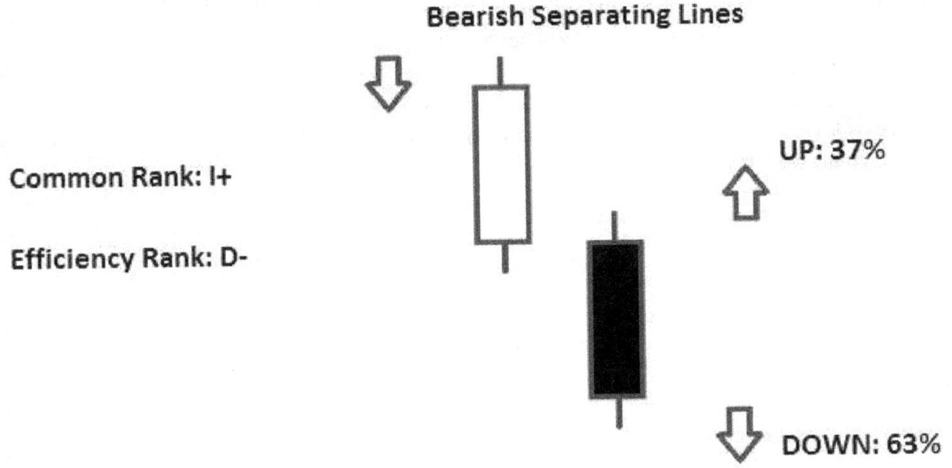

Bearish Separating Lines

Common Rank: I+

Efficiency Rank: D-

UP: 37%

DOWN: 63%

Strike in three lines

In most cases, it ought to be
You can find it in the variations: Bearish or bullish, depending on where the Trend is.

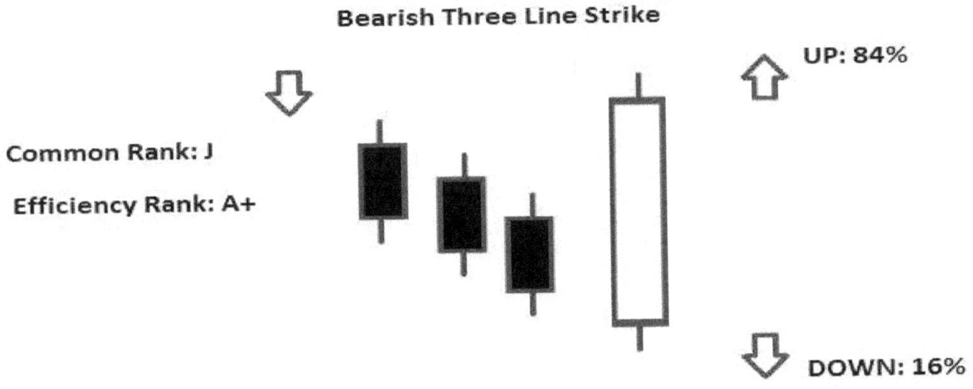

Bearish Three Line Strike

Common Rank: J

Efficiency Rank: A+

UP: 84%

DOWN: 16%

a signal of continuation of the current Trend.

During an Uptrend, it occurs; The candles that follow the Pattern require confirmation. White is used for the First, Second, and Third Candles. Additionally, the Close of each Candle is higher than the Close of the previous Candle.

The Fourth Candle is a long, black candle; It has an open that is higher than the first candle's open and a close that is lower than the first candle's open (the fourth candle fully contains the three previous candles within his real body).

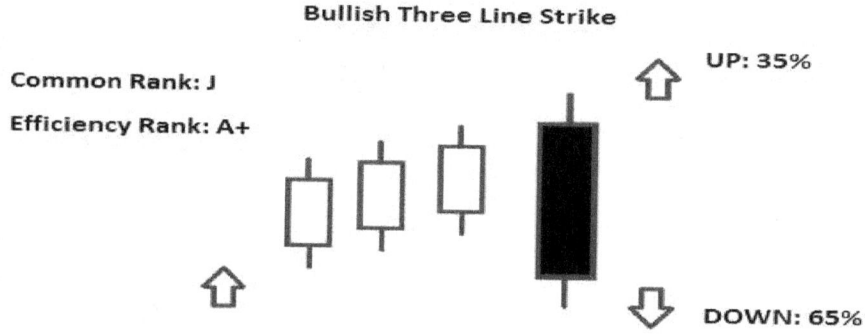

Bullish Three Line Strike

Common Rank: J

Efficiency Rank: A+

UP: 35%

DOWN: 65%

Pattern of meeting lines

During a Downtrend, it occurs; Candles that adhere to the Pattern necessitate confirmation.
The First Candle is a long, black candle.
The Second Candle is white, long; It has the Close at the same level as the First Candle's Close (More or Less).

Bullish Meeting Lines

Common Rank: H+

Efficiency Rank: B-

UP: 56%

DOWN: 44%

During an Uptrend, it occurs; Candles that adhere to the Pattern necessitate confirmation.
The Initial Candle is white and long.
The Second Candle is a long, black candle; It has the Close at the same level as the First Candle's Close (more or less)..

Bearish Meeting Lines

Common Rank: G+

Efficiency Rank: B

UP: 51%

DOWN: 49%

Play with gapping prices

Typically it ought to be a sign of continuation of the latest thing.
During a Downtrend, it occurs; Candles that adhere to the Pattern necessitate confirmation..

The First Candle is a long, black candle.
 The Real Bodies of the Second, Third, and Fourth Candles are all relatively close to the level of the Low of the First Candle.
The black, long Fifth Candle descends from the previous candle.
The "Sideways" period can last up to eleven candles (though it may only last three); These candles are referred to as spinning tops (with a brief real body).

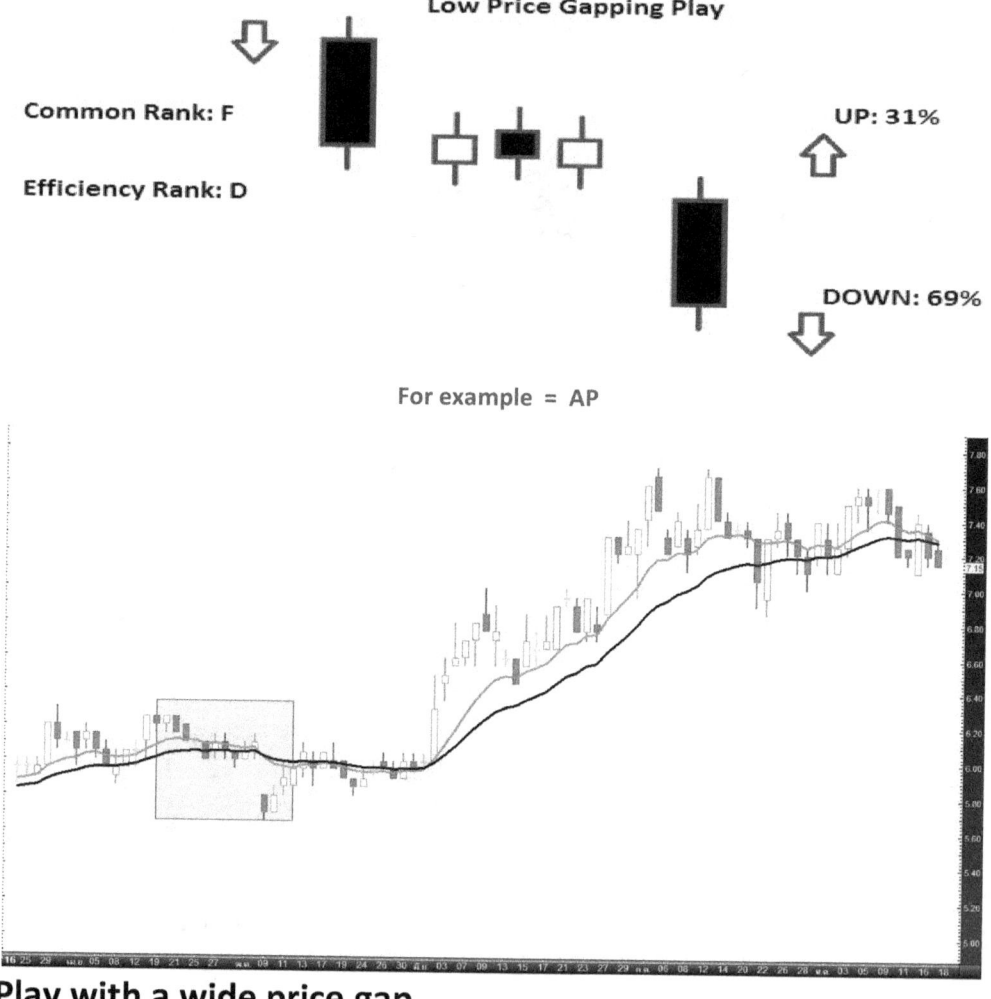

Play with a wide price gap

Normally, it should indicate that the current trend will continue.
During an Uptrend, it occurs; Candles that adhere to the Pattern necessitate confirmation.
The Initial Candle is white and long.
The Real Bodies of the Second, Third, and Fourth Candles are all relatively close to the level of the First Candle's High.

The Fifth Candle is long and white, separated from the First Candle by a gap.
The "Sideways" period can last up to eleven candles (though it may only last three); These candles are referred to as spinning tops (with a brief real body).

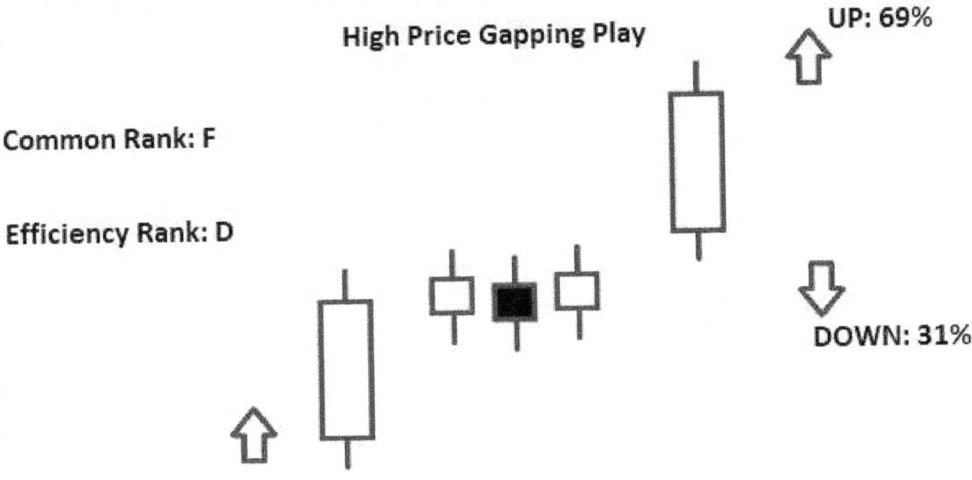

Common Rank: F

Efficiency Rank: D

Pigeon homing pattern

In most cases, it should indicate a bullish trend reversal.
During a Downtrend, it occurs; The candles that follow the Pattern require confirmation. The First Candle is black and long, while the Second Candle is shorter than the First Candle but is black. The Real Body of the First Candle houses the entire Second Candle's Real Body. Reversal of the Trend and Confirmation of the Pattern: when the Lowest Low of the Two Candles Following the "Homing Pigeon" is lower than the Close of that Candle.

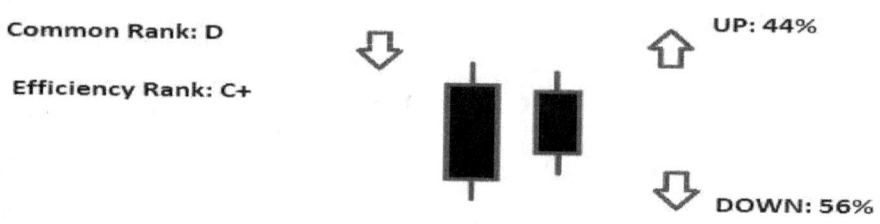

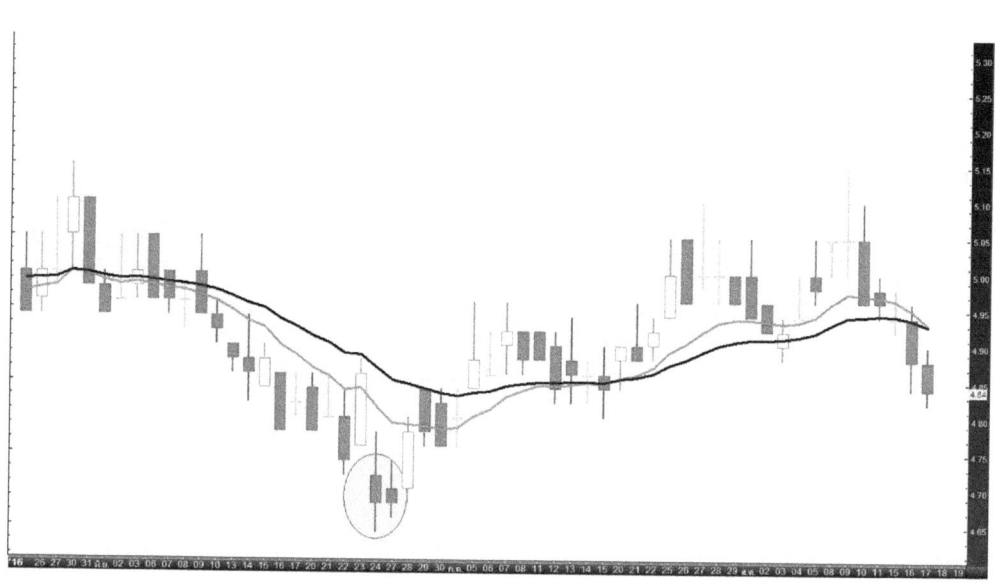

8-10-12-13 New cost lines

During an Uptrend, it occurs; Candles that adhere to the Pattern necessitate confirmation.
Eight consecutive candles, each with a higher high, define the pattern.

The Close of the previous Candle Line should be checked to confirm the Pattern once more: There is a greater likelihood that prices will rise if it is above the actual body of the previous candle. Prices are more likely to fall if the Close is lower than the top of the real body of the previous candle.

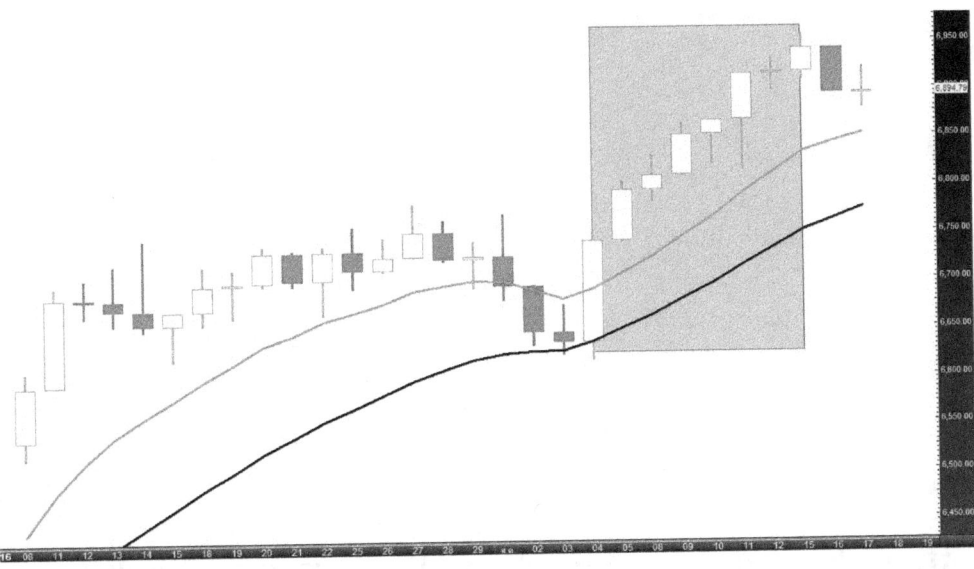

Scoop pattern

During a Sideways Trend, it occurs; Candles that adhere to the Pattern necessitate confirmation.

The spinning tops, doji, small candles, and other patterns begin to indicate the markets' indecisiveness.

(1) After that, the price begins to fall (probably as a result of traders who anticipated a rise in prices but are selling now that the trend is sideways because they no longer believe in a rise) 2) Other traders are drawn to this price drop because they anticipate a subsequent rise in prices. As a result, prices begin to rise: A new Uptrend will begin if the prices surpass the phase of uncertainty; The Pattern will fail if not. 3)

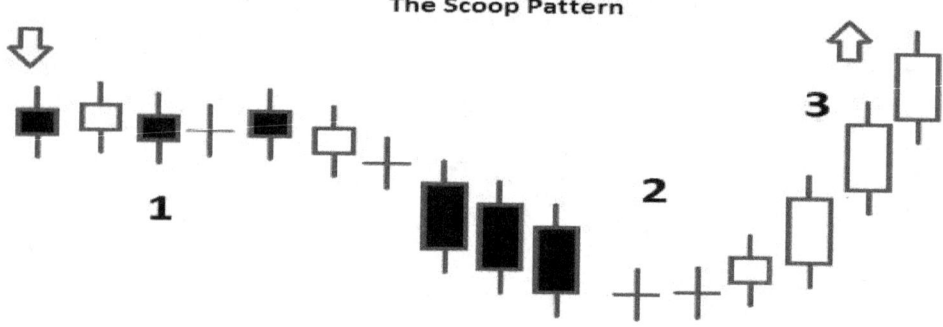

Patterns known as the J-Hook and the Inverted J-Hook

Normally, it should indicate that the current trend will continue.

It happens during an Upswing; Candles that adhere to the Pattern necessitate confirmation.

At the start of the pattern, prices rise quickly. 1) Following that, there is a Candlestick Pattern that serves as a bearish cue and prompts traders to begin selling. 2) The prices decrease before reaching a point of "indecision"; There ought to be a bullish signal at the conclusion of this phase of uncertainty. 3) The prices begin to rise and reach the Previous High, which was established by the Phase (1) In the event that the costs continue rising, going over this High, there ought to be another Upturn in Costs.

The Pattern has failed if prices do not exceed the High; The Double Top Pattern (a pattern from the technical analysis) is produced in this instance by the Pattern.

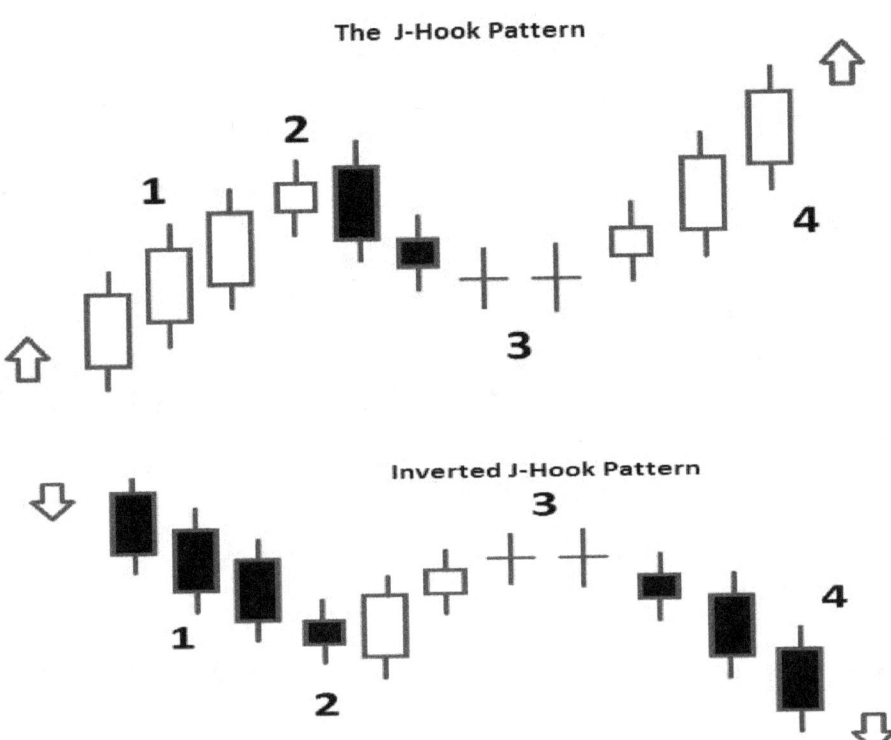

For example = KCE

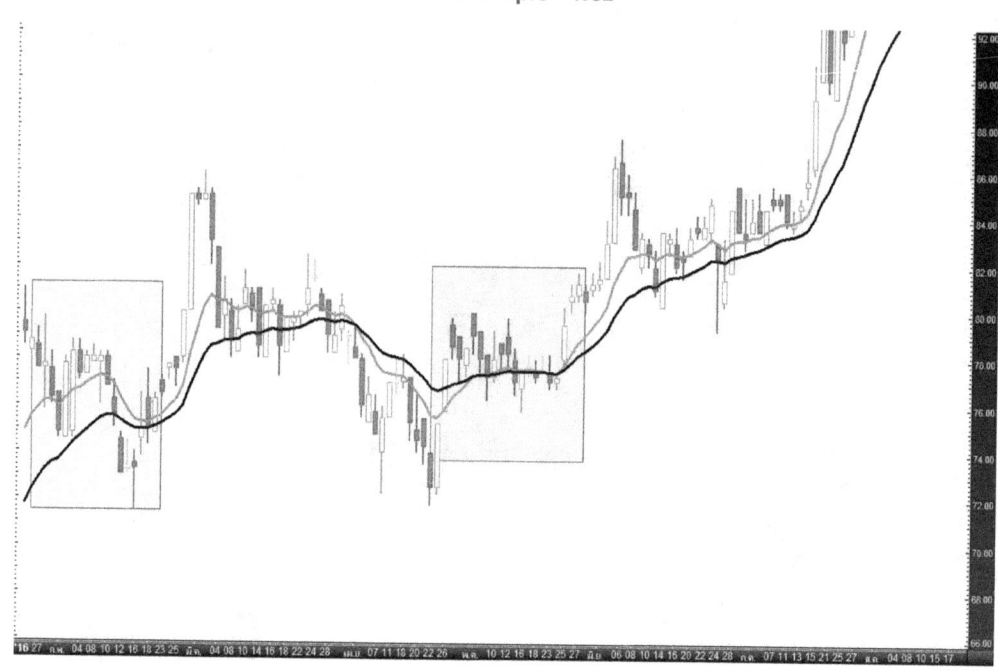

For example = SAPPE

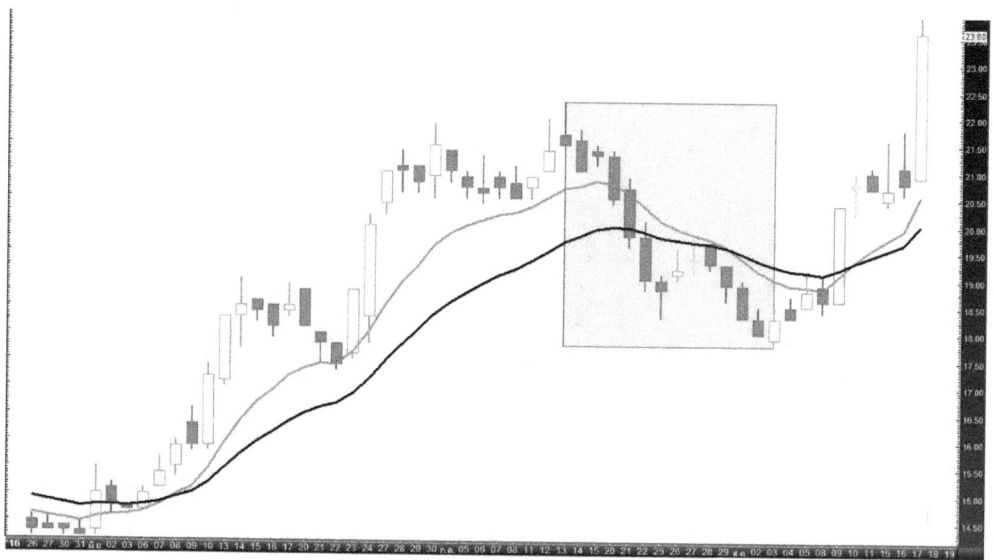

Cradle shape

Normally, it should mean that the current trend is changing.

During a Downtrend, it occurs; The candles that follow the Pattern require confirmation. Due to traders selling because they are concerned about the downtrend, the pattern begins with a long, black candle.

After that, the prices go through a period of uncertainty (there are Doji candles, spinning tops, hammers, and inverted hammers), keeping the prices in a precarious balance.

A long, white candle (which indicates the strength of the rise) marks the beginning of the pattern's price rise.

The Cradle Pattern

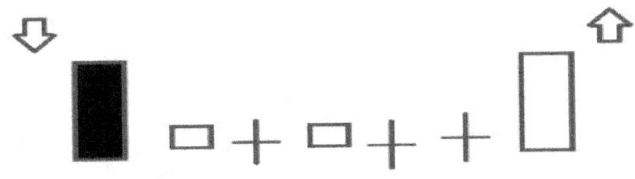

For example = SMPC

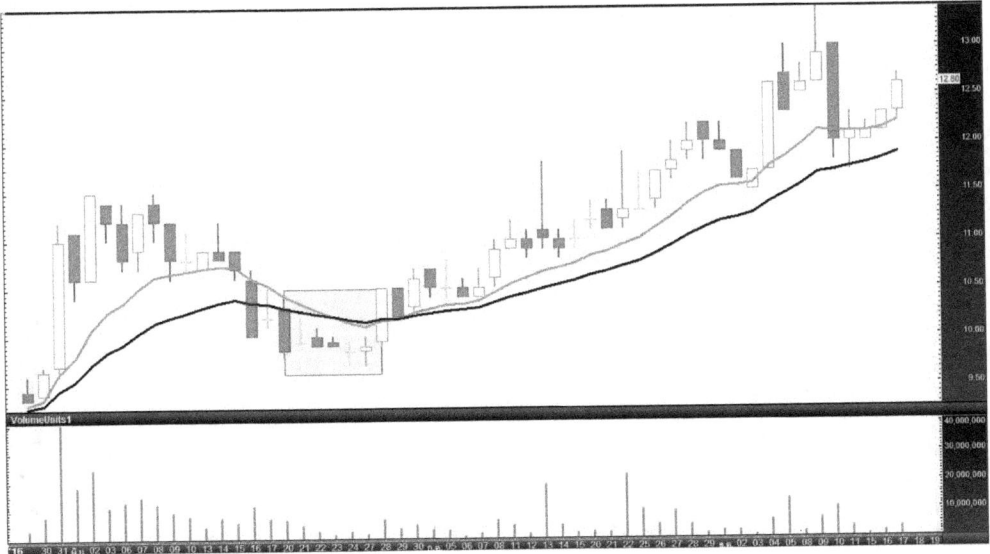

Increasing in three ways

During an Uptrend, it occurs; affirmation is expected by the candles that follow the Example. The white First and Fifth Candles are longer than the Pattern's other three candles.

The Second, Third, and Fourth Candles are all black (or their colors alternate: The fact that they symbolize a decline in prices is all that matters; Usually, the Third Candle, which can be any color, is used. Additionally, these Candles are completely contained within the First Candle's Real Body (or High-Low Range); while the Lows are higher than the First Candle's Open and the Highs are lower than the First Candle's Close.

The fifth candle's close is higher than the first candle's close.

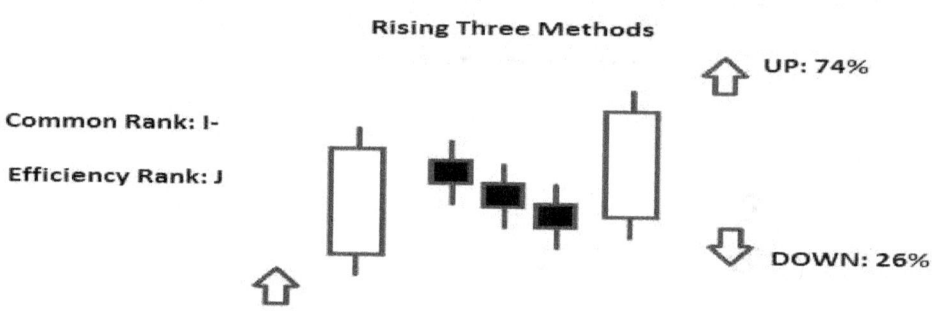

For example = SPA

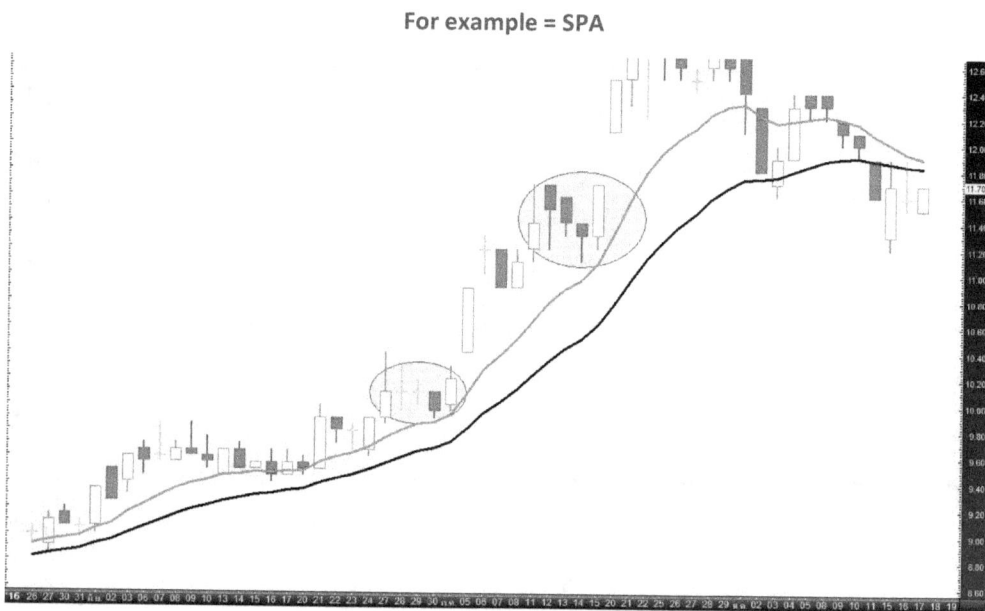

Falling in Three Ways

During a Downtrend, it occurs; Candles that adhere to the Pattern necessitate confirmation. The black First and Fifth Candles are longer than the Pattern's other three candles.

The second, third, and fourth candles are all white (or the colors alternate: They only matter because they show a rise in prices; Usually, the Third Candle, which can be any color, is used. Additionally these Candles are completely held inside the Genuine Body of the Principal Flame (or inside the High-Low Scope of the Primary Candle); while the Highs are above the Close of the First Candle and the Lows are below the First Candle's Open.

The fifth candle's close is lower than the first candle's close.

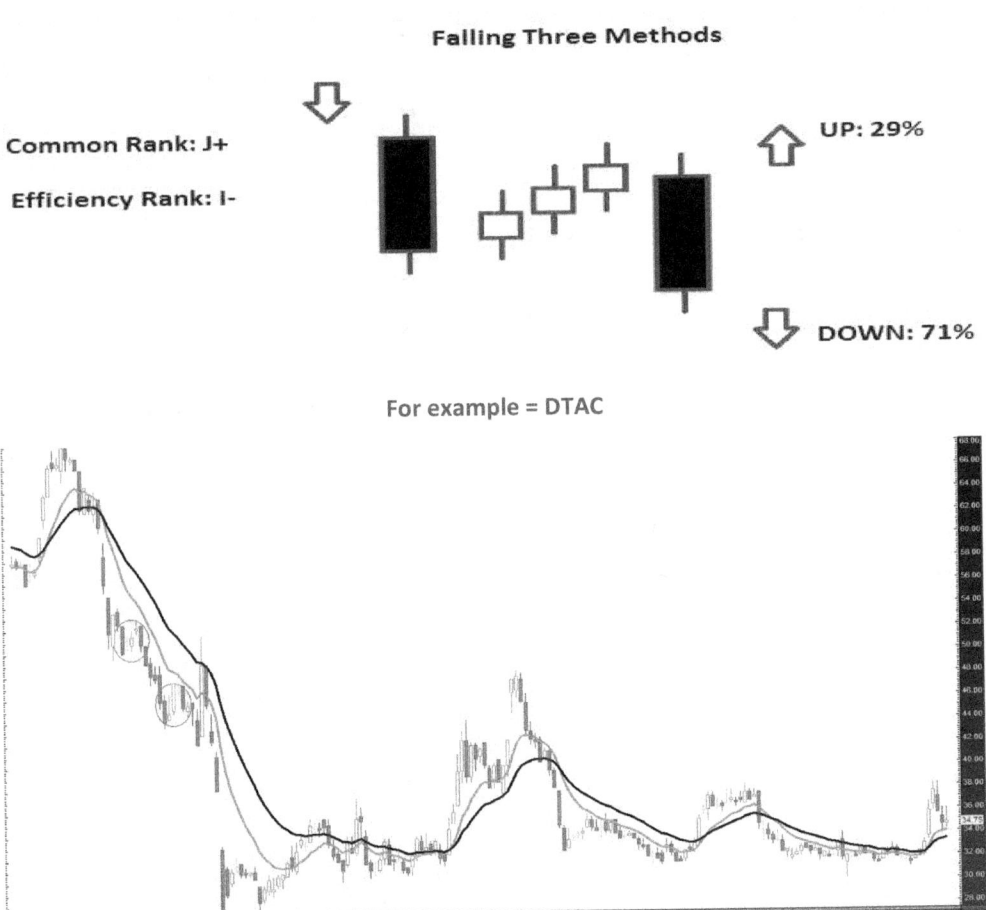

Stalled pattern or deliberate pattern

During an Uptrend, it occurs; Candles that adhere to the Pattern necessitate confirmation.
Ordinarily it ought to be a sign of Negative inversion of the latest thing.
The Example is made by Three White Candles: The Real Body of the First and Second Candles is longer than that of the Third Candle.
Each candle's Open and Close should be greater than the previous candle's Open and Close.

The Third Candle may also be a Doji Candle due to its short Real Body; also, it has an Upper Shadow extremely tall. Lastly, the Open is close to the level of the Second Candle's Close.

The affirmation of the Negative Inversion could be from the following Candles, when one of them (While is falling) defeats the midpoint of the Genuine Body of the Subsequent Flame.

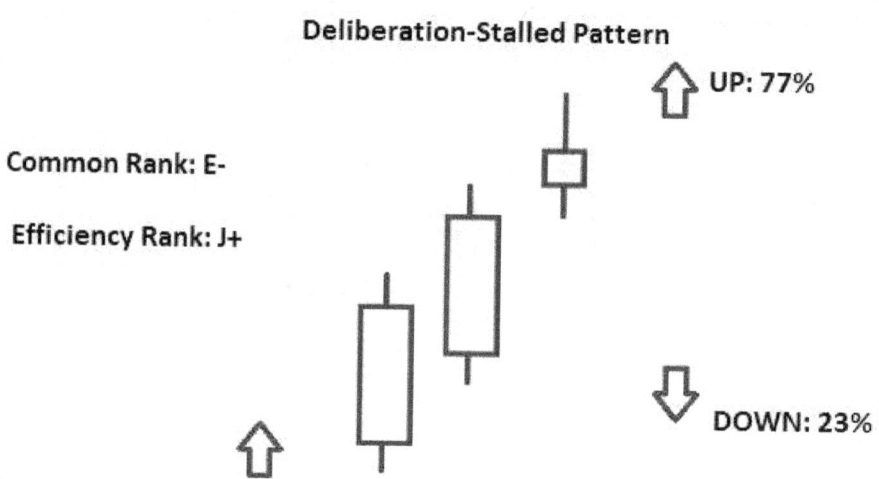

Pattern for advance blocks

During an Uptrend, it occurs; Candles that adhere to the Pattern necessitate confirmation.
In most cases, it should indicate a bearish trend reversal.
The pattern is made up of three white candles, each of which gradually has a real body that is shorter.
The Real Body of the previous candle should contain the Open of the second and third candles.
The Candles' Closes are frequently far from their respective Highs.
Particularly the Upper Shadows of the Last Two Candles, the Candles' Shadows are gradually growing taller.

When one of the subsequent candles, which is falling, surpasses the midpoint of the Real Body of the first candle, confirmation of the bearish reversal could occur.

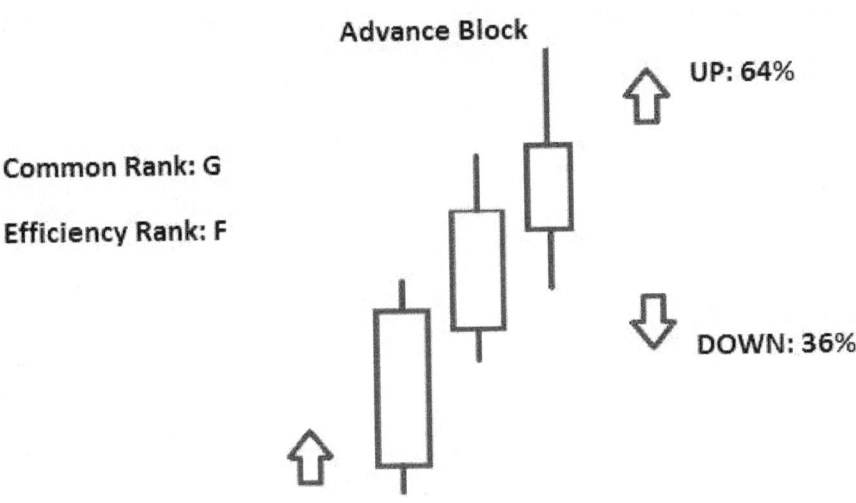

Common Rank: G

Efficiency Rank: F

Kicker

You can find in the above realistic why this example is so unstable. There is a bullish and a bearish version, as with most candle patterns. In the bullish variant, the stock is dropping down and the last red light closes at the lower part of the reach.

The stock gaps then open and close above the previous day's high the following day. This "shock event" attracts new traders on the long side and forces short sellers to cover.

In the bearish version, this is reversed.

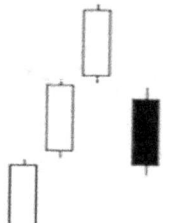

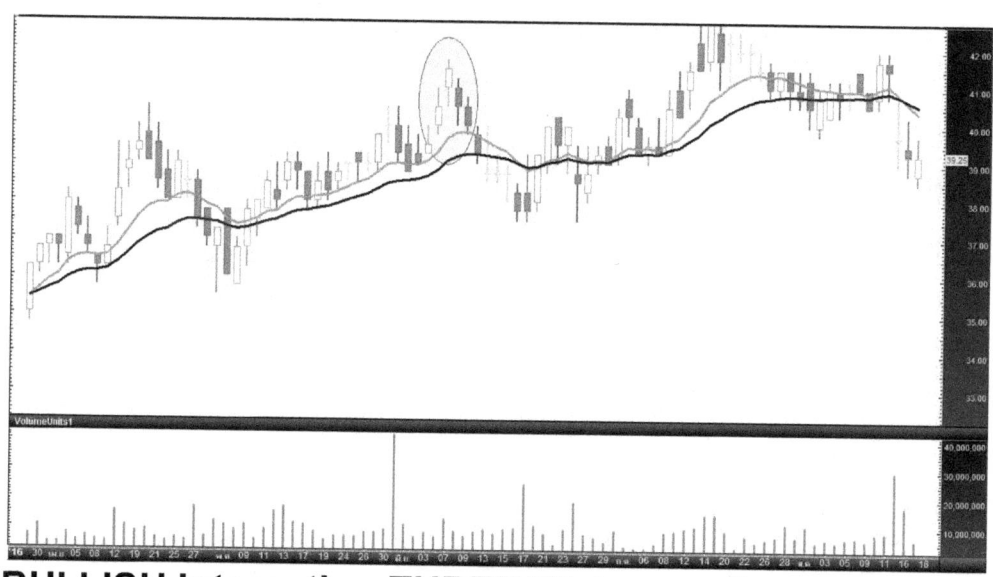

BULLISH Interesting THREE Waterway Base

Definition

This pattern has three candlesticks and has some similarities to the Bullish Morning Star. It shows up in a downtrend. The next small black body, which typically has a long lower shadow, is enveloped by the first day's black candlestick. A small white body that closes below the end of the second day completes the pattern.

Acceptance Criteria

1. The market is dominated by a downward trend.
2. On the first day, a black candlestick is observed.

3. A black body that opens higher, makes a new low, and then closes close to the high is the second day.

4. Below the second day, the third day is a brief white day.

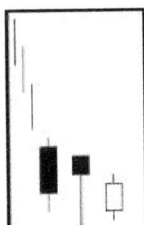

TWO RABBITS BULLISH DOWNSIDE GAP

Definition

This is a bullish reversal pattern with three candlesticks. The downside gap is represented by the gap that exists between the white body of the second day and the black body of the first day. The rabbits, ready to emerge from their burrow, are represented by the white candlesticks of the second and third days.

Acknowledgment Rules

1. A dominant downtrend characterizes the market.

2. On the first day, a normal or long black candlestick appears.

3. The second day is a brief, gaping white candlestick.

4. Another white candlestick appears on the final day, opening at or below the open and closing above the previous day's close but still below the first day's close.

Three Bullish Stars in the South

Definition

In a downtrend that is slowly deteriorating, this pattern consists of three black candlesticks that have lower closes and higher lows in succession.

Acceptance Criteria

1. A dominant downtrend characterizes the market.

2. On the first day, a black candlestick with a long lower shadow and almost no upper shadow appears.

3. Another black candlestick appears the following day, closing below the previous day's close and opening within the range of the previous day's body. However, its lowest point is higher.

4. The final day features a lower low and a small black Marubozu.

BABY SWALLOW WITH A BULLISH CONCEALER

Definition

Four black candlesticks form a pattern that looks like this. Even though the final close is at a new low, a short down day followed by a fourth black day after two falling Black Marubozu days indicates that the downtrend has significantly eroded.

Acceptance Criteria

1. The downtrend is confirmed by two falling Black Marubozu days at the beginning.

2. The third day has a downside gap and a short black. However, a long upper shadow is produced when this day trades into the body of the previous day.

3. The third day, including the shadow, is completely enveloped by the fourth black day.

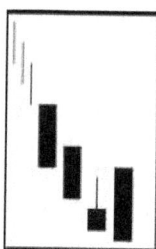

Bottom of Bullish Ladder

Definition

This is a five-candle pattern with three strong black candlesticks at the beginning. With the fourth lower close, the trend downward continues. The following day has higher gaps and closes than the previous day or two. This could suggest a bullish turn around.

Acceptance Criteria

1. A dominant downtrend characterizes the market.

2. Similar to the Three Black Crows pattern, there are three powerful black candlesticks.

3. The fourth black candlestick has a long upper shadow and also closes lower.

4. The fifth day is stark white and has an open above the body of the previous day.

Bullish following the bottom gap up

Definition

This is a five candle design that beginnings with three dark candles. The change in color at the fourth candlestick indicates a bottom reversal for the market. The reversal is confirmed by the following day's higher gaps and robust upward movement.

Acceptance Criteria

1. A dark candlestick serves as the pattern's foundation.

2. The next two days are also black days, and their closing prices are lower than those of the previous day.

3. The third day falls apart and begins shortly after the second day's end.

4. White is the fourth day.

BLOCK WITH BULLISH DESCENT

Definition

This example comprises of three sequential dark candles with successively lower shut in a downtrend. The Bearish Advanced Block Pattern complements it.

Acceptance Criteria

1. A dominant downtrend characterizes the market.

2. The first day, a black candlestick appears.

3. The next two days are black candlesticks, with each opening within the range of the previous day's body and closing below the close of the previous day.

4. The lower shadows on the last two days are long.

Requirements for the Pattern and Flexibility

A normal or long black candlestick should be the first candlestick of a bullish descent block. The following black candlesticks must close below the previous day's close and open within the range of the previous day's body. The lower shadows should get longer while the bodies of the three black candlesticks should get shorter.

BULLISH Thought BLOCK

Definition

In a downtrend, this pattern is made up of three black candlesticks that close lower each time. The Bearish Deliberation Block Pattern complements it.

Acceptance Criteria

1. The market is dominated by a downward trend.
2. The first day, a black candlestick appears.
3. Another black candlestick appears the following day, opening within the range of the previous day's body and closing below the previous day's close.
4. The final day is a spinning top, a short black candlestick, or a Doji that falls below the second day..

Requirements for the Pattern and Flexibility

The Bullish Deliberation Block's first two black candlesticks should not be shorted. The second day should open at or above the first day's close, while the second day's close should be at or below the first day's close. A Doji or a short black candlestick can form the gaping down third candlestick.

Alert for Bullish Squeeze

Definition

This is a bullish reversal pattern with three days left. It was created because prices frequently break to the upside following this pattern, particularly when the pattern is preceded by a strong move to the downside.

Acceptance Criteria

1. A dominant downtrend characterizes the market.
2. The first day, a black candlestick appears.
3. When compared to the previous day, the second and third days each have higher lows and higher highs. It matters not what color they are.
4. The three days' bodies' sizes are irrelevant.

Requirements for the Pattern and Flexibility

A black candlestick ought to be the first one. The other two candlesticks can be any color and any length, but they should have higher lows followed by lower highs.

BULLISH AFTER BOTTOM GAP UP

Definition

This is a five-candlestick pattern with three black candlesticks at the beginning. The change in color at the fourth candlestick indicates a bottom reversal for the market. The reversal is confirmed by the following day's higher gaps and robust upward movement.

Acceptance Criteria

1. A dark candlestick serves as the pattern's foundation.
2. The next two days are also black days, and their closing prices are lower than those of the previous day.
3. The third day falls apart and begins shortly after the second day's end.
4. White is the fourth day.
5. The fifth day is a strong white with a gap above the close of the previous day caused by an open.

Requirements for the Pattern and Flexibility

The initial three days of the Bullish After Base Hole Up areas of strength for are candles with sequential lower opens and lower closes. The gap down should be the third black. The gap is filled by a white candlestick on the fourth day, which opens higher. The fifth day is serious areas of strength for a candle that makes a body hole with the fourth day. This pattern does not contain any short candlesticks.

ON NECK LINE

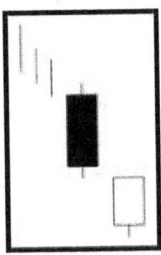

Description

The crucial word here is "almost," as the On Neck Line pattern is almost a "meeting line pattern." The ON Neck pattern does not reach the closing price of the previous day; it just arrives at the earlier day's low.

Criteria

1. In a downtrend, a long black candle forms.
2. The next day is shorter than the day before; The body, on the other hand, is typically smaller than in the meeting line pattern.
3. The second day ends at the lowest point of the first day.

Pattern Psychology

A long black candle accentuates a market's downward trend after it has been moving in that direction for some time. The following day begins lower, with a small gap down, but the trend is stopped by a move back up to the low of the previous day. The fact that there was not more strength in the up move should make buyers feel uneasy. The following day, the sellers withdraw to maintain the downward trend.

IN NECK LINE

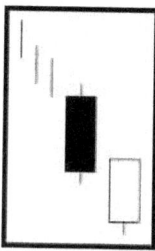

Description

The In Neck pattern has the appearance of a meeting line. The only difference between it and the On Neck pattern is that it closes slightly higher than the previous day's close. The suggestion is to confirm. The In Neck Line suggests some short covering, but not a shift in the direction of the trend.

Criteria

1. In a downtrend, a long black candle forms
2. The next day is shorter than the day before; nonetheless, the body is normally more modest than one found in the Gathering Line design.
3. The second day ends at or slightly higher than the previous day's close.

Pattern Psychology

The situation is identical to that of the On Neck pattern. A long black candle accentuates a market's downward trend after it has been moving in that direction for some time. The following day begins lower, with a small gap down, but the trend is stopped by a move back up to the low of the previous day. The fact that there was not more strength in the up move should make buyers feel uneasy. The following day, the sellers withdraw to maintain the downward trend.

THRUSTING

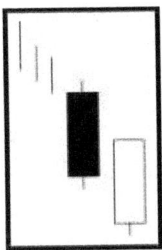

Description

The Thrusting pattern is also similar to the Meeting Line pattern, which is almost like an "On Neck" or "In Neck" pattern. The only difference between it and the "On Neck" pattern is that it closes close to but slightly below the midpoint of the black body from the previous day.

Criteria

1. In a downtrend, a long black candle forms.
2. The next day is shorter than the day before; On the other hand, the body is typically larger than in the On Neck and In Neck patterns.
3. The second day's candle closes just a little bit below its midpoint on the previous day.

Pattern Psychology

The situation is identical to that of the "On neck" pattern. A long black candle accentuates a market's downward trend after it has been moving in that direction for some time. The following day opens lower, a little hole down, yet the pattern is ended by a move back up to the earlier day's low. The fact that there was not more strength in the up move should make buyers feel uneasy. The dealers step back in the following day to proceed the downtrend. It is not quite as strong as the Piercing Line pattern, but it is stronger than the On neck and In Neck patterns.

White lines running side by side - continuation pattern

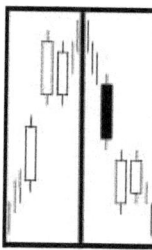

Description

One next to the other White Lines are found in upswings. Two white candles structure one next to the other in the wake of gapping up from the past white flame. In Japanese, narabi refers to "in a row." The name Narabi, or "whites in a row," When observed by themselves, black or white Side-by-Side Lines signify a pause or impasse. For this situation, the financial exchange information has an alternate importance since they happen after a hole in the pattern's heading.

Criteria

1. An uptrend is taking place. Between two candles of the same color, there is a gap.
2. The variety the initial two candles is equivalent to the predominant pattern.
3. A candle opens on the third day at the same or close to the open price of the previous day.
4. The third day ended roughly at the same time as the previous day.

ON NECK LINE

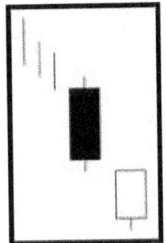

Description

The On Neck Line pattern is almost a 'meeting line pattern', but the critical term is 'almost'. The ON Neck pattern does not reach the previous day's close; it only reaches the previous day's low.

Criteria

1. A long black candle forms in a downtrend.
2. The next day gaps down from the previous day's close; however, the body is usually smaller than one seen in the meeting line pattern.
3. The second day closes at the low of the previous day.

Pattern Psychology

After a market has been moving in a downward direction, a long black candle enhances the downtrend. The next day opens lower, a small gap down, but the trend is halted by a move back up to the previous day's low. The buyers in this up move should be uncomfortable that there was not more strength in the up move. The sellers step back in the next day to continue the downtrend.

IN NECK LINE

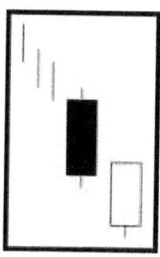

Description

The In Neck pattern is almost a Meeting Line pattern. It has the same description as the On Neck pattern except that it closes at or slightly above the previous day's close. Confirmation is suggested.
The In Neck Line indicates some short covering, but not a change in trend direction.

Criteria

1. A long black candle forms in a downtrend
2. The next day gaps down from the previous day's close; however, the body is usually smaller than one seen in the Meeting Line pattern.
3. The second day closes at the close or just slightly above the close of the previous day.

Pattern Psychology

This is the same scenario as the On Neck pattern. After a market has been moving in a downward direction, a long black candles enhances the downtrend. The next day opens lower, a small gap down, but the trend is halted by a move back up to the previous day's low. The buyers in this up move should be uncomfortable that there was not more strength in the up move. The sellers step back in the next day to continue the downtrend

THRUSTING

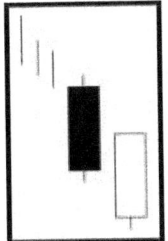

Description

The Thrusting pattern is almost an 'On Neck' or an 'In Neck' pattern and resembles the Meeting Line pattern, also. It has the same description as the 'On Neck' pattern except that it closes near, but slightly below the midpoint of the previous day's black body.

Criteria

1. A long black candle forms in a downtrend.

2. The next day gaps down from the previous day's close; however, the body is usually bigger than the ones found in the On Neck and In Neck patterns.
3. The second day closes just slightly below the midpoint of the previous day's candle.

Pattern Psychology

This is the same scenario as the 'On neck' pattern. After a market has been moving in a downward direction, a long black candle enhances the downtrend. The next day opens lower, a small gap down, but the trend is halted by a move back up to the previous day's low. The buyers in this up move should be uncomfortable that there was not more strength in the up move. The sellers step back in the next day to continue the downtrend. It is a little stronger than the On neck and In Neck patters, but not quite as strong as the Piercing Line pattern.

White lines running side by side - continuation pattern
(Narabi aka)

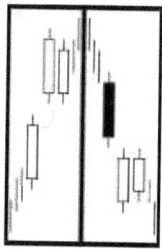

Description

Uptrends have side-by-side white lines. After gapping up from the previous white candle, two white candles form side by side. In Japanese, narabi refers to "in a row." The name Narabi, or "whites in a row," When observed by themselves, black or white Side-by-Side Lines signify a pause or impasse. Because they occur following a pause in the trend's direction, the stock market data in this instance have a different meaning.

Criteria

1. An uptrend is in progress. A gap occurs between two candles of the same co9lor.
2. The color the first two candles is the same as the prevailing trend.
3. The third day, a candle opens at the same or near the open price of the previous day.
4. The third day closed near the close of the previous day.

HOMING PIGEON

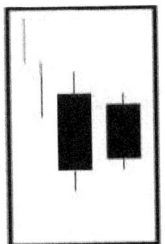

Description

Except for the color of the body on the second day, the Homing Pigeon is the same as the Harami. A two-candle formation in a market that is trending downward forms the pattern. The color of both candles matches the current trend. The pattern's first body is long, while the second body is shorter. The open and the end of the subsequent day happens inside the open and the end of the earlier day. Its presence signifies the end of the trend.

Criteria

1.The first candle has a black body; The second candle has a black body.
2.The downtrend has been obvious for quite some time. At the trend's conclusion, a lengthy black candle appears.

3.The second day opens higher than the previous day's close and closes lower than the previous day's open price but above the previous day's closing price.

4.In contrast to the Western Inside Day, only the body must remain in the body from the previous day; The Inside Day, on the other hand, requires that both the body and the shadows remain within the body of the previous day.

5.To demonstrate that the trend is ascending, additional confirmation is required for a reversal signal.

Enhanced Signals

The evidence for a reversal is stronger the higher the second candle closes above the first black candle.

Pattern Analysis

The bulls open higher than the previous close after a long black candle and a strong downtrend have occurred. The shorts begin to cover out of concern. The price ends the day lower, but not as low as it was the previous day. This provides sufficient support for the short sellers to recognize that the trend has been broken. Everyone would be persuaded that the trend was turning around by a strong day following that. Because short positions are being retracted, the volume is typically higher than the recent average.

LOW MATCHING

Description

The only difference between the Matching Low pattern and the Homing Pigeon pattern is that the two days of the pattern close on their lows at the same level. After a long downtrend, perceiving that the cost has shut at a similar level without going through is a sign to the bears that the base has been hit.

Criteria

1.The body of the primary light is dark; The second candle has a black body.

2.The downtrend has been obvious for quite some time. At the trend's conclusion, there are long black candles.

3.The second day begins higher than the previous day's close and ends the same as the previous day.

4.To demonstrate that the trend is ascending, additional confirmation is required for a reversal signal.

Pattern Analysis

The bulls open higher than the previous close after a long black candle and a strong downtrend have occurred. The shorts begin to cover out of concern. However, the bears retain sufficient control to close the price at the day's low, which is the same as the previous day's close. The fact that it could not close below the previous close has a psychological effect on bears because they are concerned that this is a support level.

www.ingramcontent.com/pod-product-compliance
Lightning Source LLC
Chambersburg PA
CBHW070316220526

45465CB00004B/1878